Guide to the Massachusetts MPJE

A Pharmacy Law Study Guide

Updated 2021

Dr. Gina Elaine Avalone, PharmD

Although the publisher and the author have made every effort to ensure that the information in this book was correct at press time and while this publication is designed to provide accurate information in regard to the subject matter covered, the publisher and the author assume no responsibility for errors, inaccuracies, omissions, or any other inconsistencies herein and hereby disclaim any liability to any party for any loss, damage, or disruption caused by errors or omissions, whether such errors or omissions result from negligence, accident, or any other cause.

Copyright © 2021 Gina Avalone

All rights reserved.

ISBN: 979-8-7185-7054-0

CONTENTS

1	FEDERAL LAW AND REGULATIONS – HISTORY	1
2	FEDERAL LAW AND REGULATIONS – MISCELLANEOUS	4
3	FEDERAL LAW AND REGULATIONS – LABELING	7
4	POISON PREVENTION PACKAGING ACT (PPPA)	11
5	FEDERAL LAW AND REGULATIONS – CONTROLLED SUBSTANCES	14
6	UNITED STATES PHARMACOPEIA (USP) COMPOUNDING	27
7	MASSACHUSETTS LAW – BOARD OF PHARMACY	31
8	MASSACHUSETTS LAW – PRESCRIPTION REQUIREMENTS	32
9	MASSACHUSETTS LAW – SCHEDULES, REFILLS, AND TRANSFERS	39
10	MASSACHUSETTS LAW – LABELING AND COUNCELLING	44
11	MASSACHUSETTS LAW – REGISTRANTS	46
12	MASSACHUSETTS LAW – PHARMACY OPERATIONS	57
13	MASSACHUSETTS LAW – MISC. PHARMACY TYPES	62
14	MASSACHUSETTS LAW – STANDING ORDERS	65
15	MASSACHUSETTS LAW – THEFT AND LOSS	68
16	MASSACHUSETTS LAW – COMPOUNDING	73
17	MASSACHUSETTS LAW – COLLABORATIVE PRACTICE	78
18	MASSACHUSETTS LAW – CONTROLLED SUBSTANCES	81
19	MASSACHUSETTS LAW – MISCELLANEOUS	85
20	REFERENCE CHARTS	90

1 FEDERAL LAW AND REGULATIONS – HISTORY

- Pure Food and Drug Act of 1906
  - Prohibited misbranding and adulteration of drugs distributed through interstate commerce
  - No requirement for ingredients or directions on manufacturer label
  - Did not include cosmetics or medical devices

- Food, Drug, and Cosmetic Act of 1938
  - Enacted due to the sulfanilamide accident
    - Anti-freeze used in a product killed 107 people
  - Required that a drug must be proven to be safe when using directions on the label
  - Label must provide adequate directions for use and warning of habit-forming ingredients
  - Cosmetics and medical devices included
  - Drugs marketed before 1938 were grandfathered in without need for above requirements
    - Includes levothyroxine, digoxin, and others

- Durham-Humphrey Amendment of 1951
  - Established 2 classes of drugs
    - "Legend" drugs
      - Needs medical supervision to be used safely
      - "Caution: Federal law prohibits dispensing without a prescription" on manufacturer label
        - Later shortened to "Rx only" in 1997

- ✓ No longer needed adequate directions for use on manufacturer label since pharmacist would be required to add a label with directions for use
- ▲ Over-the-counter (OTC)
  - ✓ Need adequate directions for use on label
- ▢ Added regulations for oral and refill prescriptions

- Kefauver-Harris Amendment of 1962 - Drug Efficacy Amendment
  - ▢ Enacted due to thalidomide concern
    - ▲ In Europe, thalidomide had caused serious birth defects
  - ▢ Drugs had to be proven both safe and effective before marketing
    - ▲ Any drugs marketed from 1938 and beyond
  - ▢ Put the Food and Drug Administration (FDA) in charge of prescription drug advertising
    - ▲ Office of Prescription Drug Promotion (OPDP)
  - ▢ Put Federal Trade Commission (FTC) in charge of OTC medication advertising
  - ▢ Added informed consent for drug trials and Good Manufacturing Practices (GMPs)

- Medical Device Amendment of 1976
  - ▢ Better classification and regulation of medical devices

- Federal Anti-Tampering Act of 1982
  - ▢ Tamper-evident packaging required for OTC products
  - ▢ Label must indicate (on somewhere other than the tamper-evident closure itself) that the packaging is tamper-evident

- Orphan Drug Act 1983
  - ▢ Incentives for creating drug for rare diseases affecting <200,000 people in the United States

- Drug Price Competition and Patent-Term Restoration Act of 1984
  - ▢ Also called Hatch-Waxman Amendment
  - ▢ Created abbreviated new drug application (ANDA) for generic medication approval
    - ▲ Only need bioequivalence proof for generics
  - ▢ Brand name drug manufacturers get up to 5 years added to patent

- Prescription Drug Marketing Act of 1987
    - Stricter regulations on drug product and sample distribution
    - Banned re-importation of prescription drug products
    - Banned sale, trade, or purchase of drug samples
    - Specified storage, handling, recordkeeping for samples
    - Barred retail pharmacies from receiving drug samples
        - Retail pharmacies may instead utilize manufacturer vouchers or coupons or starter packs

- FDA Modernization Act of 1997
    - New Drug Application (NDA) fast track
        - Expedited approval of new drugs for serious conditions
    - Clarified some compounding regulations
    - "Rx Only" replaced old language
    - "Warning - may be habit forming" language eliminated
    - Encouraged supplemental NDAs
        - Add new indications for existing drug products
    - 6 additional patent months for pediatric drugs

- Medicare Prescription Drug Improvement and Modernization Act of 2003
    - Medicare Parts A to D
        - A – hospitalization insurance
        - B – physician services
        - C – Medicare Advantage
        - D – prescription medications
            - Cannot force patients to use mail order, must allow 90-day supplies at local pharmacies
            - Medication Therapy Management (MTM)
                - Part D sponsors automatically enroll targeted patients with chronic disease on many medications
                - Pharmacists help manage those conditions by going over medications and making recommendations to providers
                - Done quarterly for participants

- United States Pharmacopeia/ National Formulary (USP/NF)
    - NOT made by the US government
    - Monographs for recognized drugs with quality standards

2 FEDERAL LAW AND REGULATIONS – MISCELLANEOUS

- Investigational New Drug application (IND)
  - After animal studies, you submit IND to FDA before you can begin human trails
    - FDA has 30 days to approve or decline the IND
- Clinical Trials
  - Phase 1
    - Healthy subjects
    - Safety, evaluate drug properties
    - Small size
  - Phase 2
    - Subjects with the disease
    - Effectiveness, dosing, adverse effects
    - 100+ subjects
  - Phase 3
    - Subjects with disease
    - Usually blinded (some patients given placebo for comparison)
    - Efficacy
    - Can be 1000s of subjects at multiple sites around the globe
  - Phase 4
    - Post marketing surveillance for more rare adverse effects
- Treatment INDs
  - Drug given to patients with life-threatening illness that are not in the trial

- New Drug Application (NDA)
  - Submitted after trials Phase 1-3 are completed
  - Takes FDA a long time (6 months+) to review
  - Once approved drug can go to market and Phase 4 begins
- Abbreviated NDA (ANDA) Hatchman-Way
  - For generics
  - Must prove bioequivalence only
  - Do not need to repeat safety and efficacy trials
- Supplemental NDA (SNDA)
  - Any change other than creating a generic
  - Can be used to add a new indication or dosage form

- Adulteration vs. Misbranding
  - Adulteration
    - Consists in whole or in part of any filthy, putrid, or decomposed substance
    - Has been prepared, packed, or held under insanitary conditions whereby it may have been contaminated with filth
    - Strength, quality, or purity differs from official compendium
    - Contains unsafe color additive
  - Misbranding
    - Labeling proves false or misleading in any way
    - Labeling missing any required elements
      - Examples: missing the name and place of business of the manufacturer, packer, or distributor or missing an accurate statement of the quantity of the contents in terms of weight, measure, or numerical count
- Recalls
  - Class I
    - Most serious
    - Reasonable probability that the use of, or exposure to, a product will cause serious adverse health consequences or death
    - Pharmacies and patients must be notified
    - Must send written notice
  - Class II
    - May cause temporary or medically reversible adverse health consequences or where the probability of serious adverse health consequences is remote
    - Pharmacy level recall
    - Must send written notice

- Class III
  - Not likely to cause adverse health consequences

- Generic Substitution
  - Electronic Orange Book
    - Contains information on which generic products are considered bioequivalent to which brand name products
    - Reference Listed Drug (RLD) = the standard used for comparison
      - Usually the original brand name medication
    - A rated = bioequivalent
      - May be substituted
    - B rated = not bioequivalent
      - May NOT be substituted
    - AB rated = meets necessary bioequivalence standards
      - May be substituted
      - When there are multiple sources designated (AB1, AB2, AB3, etc.), AB1 can only be substituted with another AB1 rated medication, etc.
  - For narrow therapeutic index (NTI) medications, variability limit is smaller than for other generics
    - IE: 5% instead of 10% difference allowable
  - For biologic medications, the term "biosimilar" is used

- Health Insurance Portability and Accountability Act (HIPAA)
  - Must provide patient with a notice when first providing service
    - No need for new notice for repeat service

3 FEDERAL LAW AND REGULATIONS – LABELING[1]

- Requirements on manufacturer containers for prescription medications
  - Name and address of the manufacturer, packer, or distributer
  - Established name of the drug
  - Quantity (weight, quantity, or dosage units)
  - Amount of active ingredient
  - "Rx Only"
  - Route if not taken orally
  - Special storage instruction if needed
  - Lot number
  - Expiration date
  - NDC code is requested but NOT required
  - Inactive additives should be listed alphabetically and separate from active ingredients
- Unit dose packaging
  - Name of the drug
  - Quantity
  - Name and address of the manufacturer, packer, or distributer
  - Lot number
  - Expiration date
- Requirements on OTC product labels "Drug Facts"
  - Active ingredients
    - Established name of each active ingredient and the quantity of each active ingredient per dosage unit

- Purpose
  - The general pharmacological categories or the principal intended actions of each active ingredient
- Uses
  - Indication(s) for the specific drug product
- Warnings
  - If applicable
    - ✓ "For external use only"
    - ✓ Reye's syndrome warning
    - ✓ "Ask a doctor before use if you have"
    - ✓ "Ask a doctor or pharmacist before use if you are"
    - ✓ Pregnancy/breast-feeding warning
    - ✓ Etc.
- Directions
  - Directions for use described in an applicable OTC drug monograph or approved drug application
- Other information
- Inactive ingredients
  - Listing of the established name of each inactive ingredient
  - Inactive ingredients shall be listed in alphabetical order
- "Questions?" or "Questions or comments?" followed by the telephone number of a source to answer questions
- Must contain the calcium content per dosage unit (e.g., tablet, teaspoonful) if the content of a single maximum recommended dose of the product is 20 mg or more
- Must contain the magnesium content per dosage unit (e.g., tablet, teaspoonful) if the content of a single maximum recommended dose of the product is 8 mg or more
- Must contain the potassium content per dosage unit (e.g., tablet, teaspoonful) if the content of a single maximum recommended dose of the product is 5 mg or more
- Must contain the sodium content per dosage unit (e.g., tablet, teaspoonful) if the content of a single maximum recommended dose of the product is 5 mg or more
  - If the amount of sodium present in the labeled maximum daily dose of the product is more than 140 milligrams: "Ask a doctor before use if you have a sodium-restricted diet"

- Special Label Warnings
  - FD&C Yellow No. 5 (tartrazine)
    - Shall bear a statement such as "Contains FD&C Yellow No. 5 (tartrazine) as a color additive"
  - Aspartame
    - Shall bear a statement to the following effect: "Phenylketonurics: Contains Phenylalanine (_) mg Per (Dosage Unit)"
  - Sulfites
    - Shall bear the warning statement "Contains (insert the name of the sulfite, e.g., sodium metabisulfite), a sulfite that may cause allergic-type reactions including anaphylactic symptoms and life-threatening or less severe asthmatic episodes in certain susceptible people"
  - Mineral oil
    - Shall bear a warning such as "Caution: To be taken only at bedtime. Do not use at any other time or administer to infants, except upon the advice of a physician."
    - Should also discourage use in pregnancy
  - Wintergreen oil (methyl salicylate)
    - >5% shall warn that use otherwise than as directed may be dangerous and that the article should be kept out of reach of children to prevent accidental poisoning
  - Sodium phosphate
    - Shall contain the sodium content per dose if the sodium content is 5 milligrams or more
    - The FDA limits the amount of sodium phosphates oral solution to not more than 90 mL (3 ounces) per OTC container
  - Ipecac Syrup
    - A statement conspicuously boxed and in red letters, to the effect: "For emergency use to cause vomiting in poisoning. Before using, call physician, the Poison Control Center, or hospital emergency room immediately for advice"
    - A warning to the effect: "Warning—Keep out of reach of children. Do not use in unconscious persons"
    - Usual dosage: 1 tablespoon (15 milliliters) in persons over 1 year of age
  - Salicylates
    - Warning about Reye's syndrome

- Alcohol Warnings (analgesics)
  - The labeling for all over-the-counter (OTC) drug products containing any internal analgesic/antipyretic active ingredients (including, but not limited to, acetaminophen, aspirin, carbaspirin calcium, choline salicylate, ibuprofen, ketoprofen, magnesium salicylate, naproxen sodium, and sodium salicylate) alone or in combination must bear a warning about use if you consume more than three alcoholic beverages a day
- Package Inserts
  - Required for prescription medications, for information only
- Patient Package Inserts (PPIs)
  - Must be provided for Accutane, statins, estrogen or progesterone containing medications
  - For inpatients, provide at initial dispensing and every 30 days

4 POISON PREVENTION PACKAGING ACT (PPPA)[2]

- Requires child-resistant closures to prevent young children from accidental poisonings on the following:
    - Acetaminophen packages >1 gram
    - Aspirin – all oral dosage forms except effervescent tablets
    - Dibucaine packages >0.5 mg
    - Diphenhydramine packages >66 mg
    - Ibuprofen packages >1 gram
    - Iron packages >250 mg
    - Ketoprofen packages >50 mg
    - Lidocaine packages >5 mg
    - Loperamide packages >0.045 mg
    - Minoxidil packages >14 mg
    - Mouthwash packages >3 grams ethanol
    - Naproxen packages >250 mg
    - All oral dosage forms of controlled substances
    - Any oral nonprescription drug that was once prescription only
    - All oral dosage forms of prescription drugs
        - See specific packaging exemptions below
        - A physician may request a certain prescription be dispensed in a non-child-resistant container
        - A patient may indicate they would like all of their prescriptions to be dispensed in non-child-resistant containers
        - These rules do not apply to prescriptions dispensed to hospital inpatients
    - An OTC with several package sizes can have one package size available without safety closures if the label states "This package for households without young children"

- When refilling a prescription, a pharmacist must use a completely new plastic container since plastic closures can lose their child-resistant features over time
    - If a glass container is used, the pharmacist need only replace the plastic top portion
- Prescription drug exemptions:
    - Sublingual dosage forms of nitroglycerin
    - Sublingual and chewable forms of isosorbide dinitrate in dosage strengths of 10 milligrams or less
    - Erythromycin ethylsuccinate granules for oral suspension and oral suspensions in packages containing not more than 8 grams of the equivalent of erythromycin
    - Cyclically administered oral contraceptives in manufacturers' mnemonic (memory-aid) dispenser packages that rely solely upon the activity of one or more progestogen or estrogen substances
    - Anhydrous cholestyramine in powder form
    - All unit dose forms of potassium supplements, including individually wrapped effervescent tablets, unit dose vials of liquid potassium, and powdered potassium in unit-dose packets, containing not more than 50 milliequivalents of potassium per unit dose
    - Sodium fluoride drug preparations including liquid and tablet forms, containing not more than 50 mg of elemental fluoride per package
    - Betamethasone tablets packaged in manufacturers' dispenser packages, containing no more than 12.6 milligrams betamethasone
    - Pancrelipase preparations in tablet, capsule, or powder form
    - Prednisone in tablet form, when dispensed in packages containing no more than 105 mg
    - Mebendazole in tablet form in packages containing not more than 600 mg of the drug
    - Methylprednisolone in tablet form in packages containing not more than 84 mg of the drug
    - Colestipol in powder form in packages containing not more than 5 grams of the drug
    - Erythromycin ethylsuccinate tablets in packages containing no more than the equivalent of 16 grams erythromycin
    - Conjugated Estrogens Tablets when dispensed in mnemonic packages containing not more than 32 mg

- Norethindrone Acetate Tablets when dispensed in mnemonic packages containing not more than 50 mg
- Medroxyprogesterone acetate tablets
- Sacrosidase (sucrase) preparations in a solution of glycerol and water
- Hormone Replacement Therapy Products that rely solely upon the activity of one or more progestogen or estrogen substances
- Colesevelam hydrochloride in powder form in packages containing not more than 3.75 grams
- Sevelamer carbonate in powder form in packages containing not more than 2.4 grams

5 FEDERAL LAW AND REGULATIONS – CONTROLLED SUBSTANCES[3]

- Controlled Substances Federal Laws
    - **Schedule I (CI)** - (A) The drug or other substance has a high potential for abuse (B) The drug or other substance has no currently accepted medical use in treatment in the United States (C) There is a lack of accepted safety for use of the drug or other substance under medical supervision
        - Examples: heroin, LSD, mescaline, peyote, MDMA
    - **Schedule II (CII)** - (A) The drug or other substance has a high potential for abuse (B) The drug or other substance has a currently accepted medical use in treatment in the United States or a currently accepted medical use with severe restrictions (C) Abuse of the drug or other substances may lead to severe psychological or physical dependence
        - Examples: cocaine, fentanyl, hydrocodone and hydrocodone combination products, methadone, amphetamine salts, methamphetamine, pentobarbital, amobarbital, secobarbital, PCP
    - **Schedule III (CIII)** - (A) The drug or other substance has a potential for abuse less than the drugs or other substances in schedules I and II (B) The drug or other substance has a currently accepted medical use in treatment in the United States (C) Abuse of the drug or other substance may lead to moderate or low physical dependence or high psychological dependence

- Examples: acetaminophen with codeine, anabolic steroids, benzphetamine, ketamine, buprenorphine, dronabinol, GHB, ≤1.8 grams of codeine per 100 ml or ≤90 mg per dosage unit of codeine, suppositories of pentobarbital, amobarbital or secobarbital
- **Schedule IV (CIV)** - (A) The drug or other substance has a low potential for abuse relative to the drugs or other substances in schedule III (B) The drug or other substance has a currently accepted medical use in treatment in the United States (C) Abuse of the drug or other substance may lead to limited physical dependence or psychological dependence relative to the drugs or other substances in schedule III
  - Examples: benzodiazepines, phenobarbital, tramadol, ~~propofol~~, modafinil, eszopiclone, carisoprodol
- **Schedule V (CV)** - (A) The drug or other substance has a low potential for abuse relative to the drugs or other substances in schedule IV (B) The drug or other substance has a currently accepted medical use in treatment in the United States (C) Abuse of the drug or other substance may lead to limited physical dependence or psychological dependence relative to the drugs or other substances in schedule IV
  - Examples: pregabalin, ≤200 mg codeine per 100 ml or 100 gm (IE: acetaminophen with codeine elixir and promethazine with codeine), Lomotil (diphenoxylate with atropine), lacosamide
- Exempt Prescription Products List
  - Certain drug products containing controlled substances are not included in these schedules as they are unlikely to be abused
    - ✓ Donnatal, Librax, Anaspaz PB, etc.
- Controlled Substance Registration
  - Valid for 3 years from issue
  - Renewal may be processed a maximum of 60 days prior to expiration
  - DEA policy allows the reinstatement of an expired registration for one calendar month after the expiration date. If the registration is not renewed within that calendar month, an application for a new DEA registration is required
    - ✓ Federal law prohibits the handling of controlled substances for any period of time under an expired registration
  - Pharmacies
    - ✓ Form 224 for initial registration, 224a for renewal

- ✓ Note: individual pharmacists do not need to register with the DEA to work in a pharmacy
- ✓ Applicant for pharmacy DEA registration does not need to be a pharmacist
- ▲ Manufacturers, distributers, importers, exporters, researchers – Form 225
- ▲ Every location needs its own DEA license
  - ✓ If you are moving locations, you need to request a modification to your license
- ▲ Registration can be suspended or revoked if the applicant:
  - ✓ Falsifies application
  - ✓ Has been convicted of a drug related felony
  - ✓ Has a state license suspended, revoked, or denied
- ▫ Ordering
  - ▲ DEA Form 222 - used to purchase or transfer CI and CII
    - ✓ Purchase from wholesaler
    - ✓ Return to supplier
    - ✓ Transfer CII from pharmacy that is closing M d,,
    - ✓ Transfer CII to a reverse distributer for destruction
    - ✓ New single-sheet forms introduced in 2019
      - ▪ DEA no longer issues triplicate forms. Triplicate DEA Forms 222 will not be accepted after October 30, 2021
    - ✓ The purchaser must make a copy of the original DEA Form 222 for its records and then submit the original to the supplier
      - ▪ The purchaser does not have the option of retaining the original
      - ▪ When the items are received, the purchaser must document on the purchaser's copy the actual number of commercial or bulk containers received and the date received
    - ✓ Controlled Substance Ordering System (CSOS) - electronic substitute for DEA Form 222 when ordering Schedule I or II substances online
      - ▪ Uses digital signature
    - ✓ Must be registered to handle CI or CII to obtain order forms from the DEA
    - ✓ Must be signed by the person who signed the most recent DEA application or by a person authorized to sign by a Power of Attorney

- Power of Attorney (POA)
  (i) Must be signed by the same person who signed the most recent application for registration or renewal registration of the CSR, the individual being given POA, and 2 additional witnesses
  (ii) May be revoked at any time by the person who granted the POA and 2 witnesses
  (iii) If someone else signs a registration renewal, need to create a new POA
- Must be filed with the executed 222 order forms and retained for as long as the order forms

✓ Order forms must be retained on site and for 2 years
- Electronic forms must be readily retrievable

✓ Supplier can refuse to fill if there is an issue with the form or an electronic signature issue
- Supplier may reject and return paper form to purchaser with a written notice of rejection or send this notice digitally for CSOS order
- Supplier nor purchaser can correct defective order, a new order is needed
- Purchaser must keep unaccepted or defective forms with a statement attached

✓ Supplier can cancel part or all of an order by crossing out drug name and writing "canceled"

✓ DEA policy does not preclude the substitution of identical products differing in packaging size from those initially ordered, provided that the actual quantity received does not exceed the amount initially ordered and that the National Drug Code number reflected is that of the actual product shipped

✓ Supplier can partially fill an order within 60 days of order

✓ Supplier can only ship to registered location

✓ Whenever any used or unused order forms are stolen or lost, this must be reported immediately to the Special Agent in charge of the DEA
- Try to identify serial numbers or date received forms
- If found, notify DEA immediately

✓ Unused order forms must be returned to the DEA if not needed

- For CIII-V DEA form 222 does not need to be used
  - The registrant must keep a receipt (invoice or packing slip) on which it records the date the drugs were received and confirm that the order is accurate
  - These receipts must be maintained either separately from all other records of the registrant or in such a way that the information required is readily retrievable
- Controlled substance prescriptions must be kept for (at least) 2 years per federal law
- Detoxification or maintenance treatment
  - Need special registration to treat opioid-dependent patients
  - SUPPORT for Patients and Communities Act of 2018
    - Allows a pharmacy to deliver a controlled substance to a practitioner for the purpose of administering the controlled substance by the practitioner if:
      - The controlled substance is delivered by the pharmacy to the prescribing practitioner at the location listed on the practitioner's certificate of registration
      - The controlled substance is to be administered for the purpose of maintenance or detoxification treatment and the practitioner who issued the prescription is a "Qualifying Practitioner" or "Qualifying Other Practitioner" and the controlled substance is to be administered by injection or implantation
      - The prescription is not issued to supply any practitioner with a stock of controlled substances for the purpose of general dispensing to patients
- Oral prescription for CII
  - For emergency situation only
    - Limited to amount of medication needed to cover emergency
  - Within 7 days of emergency prescription, prescriber must deliver a written prescription to the pharmacist stating "Authorization for Emergency Dispensing" and the date of the oral order
  - Must notify the DEA if the prescriber fails to deliver the written follow up
- Faxed prescription for CII
  - In order to expedite the filling of a prescription, a prescriber may transmit a schedule II prescription to the pharmacy by facsimile. The original schedule II written prescription must be presented to the pharmacist and verified against the facsimile

- at the time the controlled substance is actually dispensed (if written prescription is allowed by state law)
  - Federally legal for home infusion pharmacies receiving prescriptions for parenteral administration, long term care facility prescriptions, hospice patient prescriptions including home hospice to use faxed CII as the written prescription
- Partial Fill
  - Federally legal to partial fill CIII-V
  - Comprehensive Addiction and Recovery Act of 2016 (CARA)
    - Created a new partial dispensing exception
    - Permits the partial dispensing of CII prescriptions at the request of the patient or the prescribing practitioner if all the following criteria are met:
      - The partial filling is not prohibited by state law
      - The prescription is written and filled in accordance with the CSA, DEA regulations, and state law
      - The total quantity dispensed in all partial fillings does not exceed the total quantity prescribed; and
      - The remaining portions of a partially filled prescription shall be filled not later than 30 days after the date on which the prescription was written
- Refills
  - CII – no refills allowed
    - An individual practitioner may issue multiple prescriptions authorizing the patient to receive a total of up to a 90-day supply of a CII controlled substance provided:
      - Each prescription must be separate
      - The individual practitioner must provide written instructions on each prescription (other than the first prescription, if the prescribing practitioner intends for that prescription to be filled immediately) indicating the earliest date on which a pharmacy may fill each prescription
      - The individual practitioner concludes that providing the patient with multiple prescriptions in this manner does not create an undue risk of diversion or abuse
      - The issuance of multiple prescriptions is permissible under applicable state laws
  - CIII and CIV – federal law states a maximum of 5 refills in a 6-month period if authorized by the prescriber
    - See MA chapter for exceptions for out-of-state providers

- ▲ Pharmacist must record (electronically or on the back of the script)
  - ✓ The name of the controlled substance, the date of refill, the quantity dispensed, the dispensing pharmacist's identification code or name/initials for each refill, and the total number of refills dispensed to date for that prescription
- ▲ If the system provides a hard copy printout of each day's controlled substance prescription refills, each pharmacist who refilled those prescriptions must verify his/her accuracy by signing and dating the printout as he/she would sign a check or legal document
- ▲ In lieu of such a printout, the pharmacy must maintain a bound logbook or a separate file in which each pharmacist involved in the day's dispensing signs a statement, verifying that the refill information entered into the computer that day has been reviewed by him/her and is correct as shown
- ▲ A pharmacy's electronic system must have the capability of printing out any refill data, which the pharmacy must maintain under the CSA. For example, this would include a refill-by-refill audit trail for any specified strength and dosage form of any controlled substance, by either brand or generic name or both, dispensed by the pharmacy
- ▫ Labeling
  - ▲ CII-IV
    - ✓ "Caution: federal law prohibits the transfer of this drug to any person other than the patient for whom it was prescribed"
  - ▲ If prescription is filled at a central fill pharmacy, the central fill pharmacy must affix to the package a label showing the retail pharmacy name and address and a unique identifier (IE: central fill pharmacy's DEA number) indicating the script was filled at the central fill pharmacy

- Transfers between Registrants
  - CI-II use DEA Form 222
  - CIII-V must be documented in writing to show the drug name, dosage form, strength, quantity, and date transferred
  - When transferring business to another registrant
    - Must notify DEA at least 14 days in advance of the date of the proposed transfer
    - On the day the controlled substances are transferred, a complete inventory must be taken and a copy of the inventory must be included in the records of both the person transferring the business and the person acquiring the business
      - This inventory will serve as the final inventory for the registrant going out of business and initial inventory for the registrant acquiring the controlled substances
        - (i) It is not necessary to send a copy of the inventory to the DEA unless requested
        - (ii) Both parties must keep a copy of this inventory for at least 2 years
  - Disposal
    - A pharmacy may transfer controlled substances to a DEA registered reverse distributor who handles the disposal of controlled substances
    - The DEA registered reverse distributor who will destroy the controlled substances is responsible for submitting a DEA Form 41 (Registrants Inventory of Drugs Surrendered) to the DEA when the controlled substances have been destroyed
      - A DEA Form 41 should not be used to record the transfer of controlled substances between the pharmacy and the reverse distributor disposing of the drugs
    - Secure and Responsible Drug Disposal Act of 2010
      - Allows authorized manufacturers, distributors, reverse distributors, narcotic treatment programs, hospitals/clinics with an on-site pharmacy, and retail pharmacies to collect pharmaceutical controlled substances from ultimate users by voluntarily administering mail-back programs and maintaining collection receptacles
      - Also allows authorized hospitals/clinics and retail pharmacies to voluntarily maintain collection receptacles at LTCFs

- Ultimate users are able to deliver unused pharmaceutical controlled substances to appropriate entities for disposal in a safe and effective manner consistent with effective controls against diversion
  (i) Receptacle must be in a secure monitored location
- Retail pharmacies and hospitals/clinics with on-site pharmacies may modify their registrations to obtain authorization to be a collector
- Only those controlled substances listed in schedule II, III, IV, or V that are lawfully possessed by an ultimate user or other authorized non-registrant person may be collected
- An LTCF may dispose of controlled substances in schedules II, III, IV, and V on behalf of an ultimate user who resides, or has resided, at such LTCF by transferring those controlled substances into an authorized collection receptacle located at that LTCF
  (i) When disposing of such controlled substances by transferring those substances into a collection receptacle, such disposal shall occur immediately, but no longer than three business days after the discontinuation of use by the ultimate user
- Distribution of stock between pharmacies
  - "Five Percent Rule" - total number of dosage units of all controlled substances distributed by a pharmacy may not exceed five percent of all controlled substances dispensed by the pharmacy during a calendar year. If at any time the controlled substances distributed exceed five percent, the pharmacy is required to register as a distributor
- Transferring prescriptions
  - A DEA registered pharmacy may transfer prescription information for schedules III, IV, and V controlled substances to another DEA registered pharmacy for the purpose of <u>refill dispensing</u> between pharmacies, on a one-time basis only
    - However, pharmacies electronically sharing a real-time, on-line database may transfer up to the maximum refills permitted by law and the prescriber's authorization
    - The original and transferred prescription(s) must be maintained for a period of two years from the date of last refill
  - Unfilled CII-V prescriptions can be forwarded electronically to another pharmacy if technology allows

- Inventories
  - Inventories and records of CII must be separate from all other schedules
  - Records must be kept for at least 2 years from the date of the inventory at the registered location
  - Inventory must be taken at open or close of business and this must be indicated on the inventory
  - Must take an inventory on the day you first engage in business even if you do not have any controlled substances on hand yet
  - After the initial inventory, registrant must take an inventory every 2 years
  - Must include
    - ✓ The date of the inventory
    - ✓ Whether the inventory was taken at the beginning or close of business
    - ✓ The name of each controlled substance inventoried
    - ✓ The finished form of each of the substances (e.g., 10 milligram tablet)
    - ✓ The number of dosage units or volume of each finished form in the commercial container (e.g., 100 tablet bottle or 3 milliliter vial)
    - ✓ The number of commercial containers of each finished form (e.g., four 100 tablet bottles)
    - ✓ The total count of the substance
  - DEA recommends, but does not require, an inventory record include the name, address, and DEA registration number of the registrant, and the signature of the person or persons responsible for taking the inventory
  - When a substance that is non-controlled is changed to a controlled substance, you must take an inventory of that substance on the date the change is made official
  - For CI and CII
    - ✓ Record exact count of each substance
  - For CIII, IV, V
    - ✓ Estimated count for open bottles unless the container holds more than 1,000 tablets or capsules in which case you must do an exact count

- DEA Numbers
  - First Letter
    - A, B, F
      - Physicians, dentists, veterinarians
    - M
      - Mid-level practitioners
  - Second Letter
    - First initial of last name or business name
  - 7-digit number with last digit as verification
    - Add the first, third, and fifth number
    - Add the second, forth, and sixth number and multiply total by 2
    - Add the results of both calculations
    - The last digit of the final sum is the 7th digit of a valid DEA number
  - Certain hospital employees (IE: interns, residents) may prescribe controlled substances under the hospital's DEA number provided that the hospital assigns a specific internal code number to each authorized practitioner and keeps a current list of these codes
  - Federal government practitioners do not need to obtain a DEA number but must state the branch of service or agency (e.g., "U.S. Army" or "Public Health Service") and the service identification number of the issuing official in lieu of the registration number required on prescription forms
- Theft or Significant Loss
  - Should a theft or significant loss of any controlled substance occur at a pharmacy, the following procedures must be implemented within one business day of the discovery of the theft or loss
  - A pharmacy must notify in writing the local DEA Diversion Field Office within one business day of discovery of a theft or significant loss of a controlled substance
    - A pharmacy must also complete a DEA Form 106 (Report of Theft or Loss of Controlled Substances) which can be found online
      - The DEA Form 106 is used to document the actual circumstances of the theft or significant loss and the quantities of controlled substances involved

- The DEA Form 106 must include the following information:
  - (i) Name and address of the firm (pharmacy)
  - (ii) DEA registration number
  - (iii) Date of theft or loss (or when discovered if not known)
  - (iv) Name and telephone number of local police department (if notified)
  - (v) Type of theft (e.g., night break-in, armed robbery)
  - (vi) List of identifying marks, symbols, or price codes (if any) used by the pharmacy on the labels of the containers
  - (vii) A listing of controlled substances missing, including the strength, dosage form, and size of container (in milliliters if liquid form) or corresponding National Drug Code numbers
- If, after the initial notification to DEA, the investigation of the theft or loss determines no such theft or loss of controlled substances occurred, a DEA Form 106 does not need to be filed. However, the registrant must notify DEA in writing of this fact in order to resolve the initial report and explain why no DEA Form 106 was filed regarding the incident
- In-transit loss is the responsibility of the supplier as long as the pharmacy does not sign for or take custody of the shipment
  - ✓ If the pharmacy does sign for or take custody of the shipment before discovering a loss then the pharmacy must submit Form 106
  - ✓ Central Fill
    - When a central fill pharmacy contracts with private, common or contract carriers to transport filled prescriptions to a retail pharmacy, the central fill pharmacy is responsible for reporting the in-transit loss upon discovery of such loss by use of a DEA Form 106
    - When a retail pharmacy contracts with private, common or contract carriers to retrieve filled prescriptions from a central fill pharmacy, the retail pharmacy is responsible for reporting in-transit losses upon discovery using a DEA Form 106
- Records
  - All required records concerning controlled substances must be maintained for at least two years for inspection and copying by duly authorized DEA officials

- Records and inventories of CII controlled substances must be maintained separately from all other records of the registrant
- All records and inventories of CIII, IV, and V controlled substances must be maintained either separately from all other records or in such a form that the information required is readily retrievable from the ordinary business records
- Must maintain:
  - ✓ DEA Form 222
  - ✓ Power of Attorney
  - ✓ Receipts and invoices for CIII-V
  - ✓ All inventory records (initial and biennial)
  - ✓ Records of substances distributed and dispensed
  - ✓ Theft or loss reports (Form 106)
  - ✓ Inventory of drugs surrendered for disposal
  - ✓ Records of transfers between pharmacies
  - ✓ DEA registration
- If a prescription is created, signed, transmitted, and received electronically, all records related to that prescription must be retained electronically
- Electronic records must be maintained electronically for two years from the date of their creation or receipt
- Financial and shipping records can be kept at a central location with DEA approval

□ Scheduled Listed Chemical Products
  - Nonprescription drugs that contain ephedrine or pseudoephedrine
  - Requirement of regulated sellers to place the products behind the counter or in locked cabinets
  - Required an individual to present an identification card that includes a photograph and is issued by a State or the Federal Government to purchase
  - The regulated seller must self-certify to DEA on an annual basis. It is the responsibility of the regulated seller to ensure that all employees have been trained prior to self-certifying
  - Quantity limit that may be sold to an individual in a day is 3.6 grams of the chemical (base)
  - For individuals, purchases in a 30-day period are limited to 9 grams, of which not >7.5 grams may be imported by means of a common or contract carrier or the U.S. Postal Service
  - A written report of losses must be filed within 15 days after the pharmacist becomes aware of the loss or theft

6 UNITED STATES PHARMACOPEIA (USP) COMPOUNDING 795 AND 797

- NOTE: USP has postponed changes to 795/797 until further notice
  - In the interim USP 795 (last revised 2014) and USP 797 (last revised 2008) remain official
- USP 795 – Non-sterile Compounding
  - Beyond use dating
    - Non-aqueous liquid and solids – 6 months
    - Aqueous solutions – 14 days when refrigerated
    - For all others – maximum of 30 days
- USP 797 - Sterile Compounding
  - ISO Classes
    - ISO Class 5
      - <3520 particles $\geq$0.5um per m^3
      - Primary Engineering Control (PEC) must be ISO Class 5
        - Laminar airflow workbench (LAFW)
          - (i) Traditional "hood" that blows clean air onto product and worker
          - (ii) Does not protect the worker from the product
        - Biological safety cabinet (BSC)
          - (i) Barrier between worker and product to protect the worker
        - Compounding aseptic isolator (CAI)
          - (i) Also called a "glove box"
          - (ii) Protects product, not worker
        - Compounding aseptic containment isolator (CACI)
          - (i) Also called a "glove box"
          - (ii) Protects both product and worker

- ISO Class 7
  - <352,000 particles ≥0.5um per m³
  - Secondary Engineering Control (SEC) also called the buffer room must be ISO Class 7
    - Room the PEC is contained in
  - Ante rooms for negative pressure buffer rooms also must be ISO Class 7 because air will flow into the buffer room
- ISO Class 8
  - <3,520,000 particles ≥0.5um per m³
  - Ante rooms for positive pressure buffer rooms
    - Room leading to buffer room
    - For hand washing, garbing, etc.
- Unclassified air
  - Normal room air, no particle limit
  - Segregated compounding area (SCA) can have unclassified air
    - Must be out of high traffic area
    - You can use a CAI or CACI in a SCA but the beyond use time is a maximum of 12 hours

□ Types of pressure
- Positive pressure room
  - Air and particles flow out, outside air does not flow in
  - Examples: SEC, ante room
- Negative pressure room
  - Vented to the outside, air flows inside, particles flow inside and out the vents
    - This is why an ante room for a negative pressure room must be ISO Class 7 because you do not want dirty air flowing inside
      (i) Examples: hazardous medication preparation room

□ Cleaning
- At the beginning of each shift, before each batch, every 30 minutes while compounding, after spills, when surface contamination is suspected
  - Primary Engineering Control
- Daily
  - Counters, surfaces, floors
- Monthly
  - Walls, ceilings, storage shelves

- Monitoring
  - Daily
    - Temperatures
      - Clean room temperature
        - (i) Less than 20 degrees Celsius
        - (ii) Less than 68 degrees Fahrenheit
      - Normal room temperature
        - (i) 20 to 25 degrees Celsius
        - (ii) 68 to 77 degrees Fahrenheit
      - Refrigerator (cold) temperature
        - (i) 2 to 8 degrees Celsius
        - (ii) 36 to 46 degrees Fahrenheit
      - Freezer (frozen) temperature
        - (i) -25 to -10 degrees Celsius
        - (ii) -13 to 14 degrees Fahrenheit
    - Humidity
      - Relative humidity <60% for clean rooms
    - Room pressure differentials
      - Positive
        - (i) At least 0.02 inches water column
      - Negative
        - (i) Negative 0.01 to 0.03 inches water column
  - Every 6 months
    - Viable and nonviable particle count
    - Viable surface samples
- Types of compounds and beyond use dating (BUD)
  - Compounded outside of a PEC
    - Immediate use
    - Used in emergencies for preparations needed immediately
  - Compounded in a PEC located in a SCA
    - Low risk compounding only
    - 12-hour BUD
  - Compounded in a PEC located in SEC
    - Low risk
      - All sterile ingredients
      - Each container including the final container cannot be entered more than twice
    - Medium risk
      - All sterile ingredients
      - Multiple doses for multiple patients or for the same patient on multiple occasions
      - Complex manipulations (IE: making TPN, eye drops)

- ✓ High risk
  - May start with non-sterile ingredients if terminal sterilization will take place
- ✓ BUD Chart

Type of Compound	BUD at Room Temperature	BUD Refrigerated	BUD Frozen
Immediate Use	1 hour	N/A	N/A
Low Risk with 12-hour BUD	12 hours	12 hours	N/A
Low Risk	48 hours	14 days	45 days
Medium Risk	30 hours	9 days	45 days
High Risk	24 hours	3 days	45 days

7 MASSACHUSETTS LAW – BOARD OF PHARMACY

Board of Pharmacy Reference Chart

Total number of members	13
Pharmacist members (total)	8
Years of experience for pharmacist members	7
Independent pharmacist members	2
Chain pharmacist members	2
Hospital pharmacist members	1
Long term care pharmacist members	1
Sterile compounding pharmacist members	1
Academia pharmacist members	1
Pharmacy technician members	1
Years of experience for pharmacy technician members	7
Representative of the public with experience in health care service delivery, administration or consumer advocacy	1
Physician members	1
Nurse members	1
Expert in patient safety and quality improvement members	1
Total term length for members (years)	3
Length of term for board president and secretary (years)	1

8 MASSACHUSETTS LAW – PRESCRIPTION REQUIREMENTS

- Who can issue prescriptions[4]
  - Physicians (including ophthalmologists, psychiatrists, etc.)
  - Dentists
  - Podiatrists
  - Veterinarians
  - Optometrists
    - Only CVI topical medications for treatment of ocular conditions except glaucoma
  - Mid-level providers
    - Pursuant to guidelines mutually developed and agreed upon by the mid-level and the supervising physician
      - ✓ Physician assistant
      - ✓ Certified nurse practitioner
      - ✓ Psychiatric clinical nurse specialist
      - ✓ Certified nurse anesthetists
    - NOTE: a clinical nurse specialist (CNS) is not authorized to prescribe
  - Nurse midwife
    - If working for a health system and has a clinical relationship with an OB/GYN
  - An intern, fellow, medical officer, alien physician, registered nurse, licensed practical nurse, or other authorized person may administer, prescribe or dispense under the registration of the registered health facility by which such person is employed, in lieu of being registered himself or herself provided that:
    - Such dispensing is done in the usual course of his business or professional practice

- The hospital or other registered health facility by whom he is employed has verified with the appropriate Board of Registration, if applicable, that the person is permitted to dispense controlled substances within Massachusetts
- Such person is acting only within the scope of his employment in the hospital or other registered health facility
- The hospital or other registered health facility authorizes the person to dispense controlled substances under the registration number of the hospital or other registered health facility and designates a specific internal code to consist of a numeric suffix to the health facility registration number preceded by a hyphen for each such person so authorized
- The hospital or other registered health facility maintains a current list of internal codes and makes such codes available at all times to other registrants, the Commissioner, and authorized law enforcement agencies

- All prescriptions must be sent electronically starting January 1, 2020
  - There is a 1-year grace period to comply for all registrants
  - Permanent exceptions beyond January 1, 2021 include:
    - Prescriptions issued by veterinarians
    - Prescriptions issued during temporary technological or electrical failure
      - IE: power outage, transmission failure, etc.
    - A time-limited waiver process for practitioners who demonstrate economic hardship or technological limitations that are not reasonably within the control of the practitioner
      - Valid reason you cannot electronically prescribe (e-scribe), must renew waiver annually
      - Should apply for waiver only for shortest time period needed
        - For example, if you know e-scribe will be implemented soon only apply for waiver for time frame until you estimate it will be ready
    - Emergency situations
      - If there is no other possibility and the patient urgently needs the medication
    - If script cannot be sent electronically due to state or federal laws
      - IE: if a prescription needs an additional document and you can't attach it electronically
    - Out-of-state prescribers or those by Veterans' Administration or Indian Health Service

- Expedited Partner Therapy for chlamydia
  - Since you do not have the partner's information
- Compounded medications
  - May be sent electronically but do not have to be
- Schedule VI medication prescriptions
- Durable Medical Equipment prescriptions
- Prescriptions for nursing home residents
  - Until 01/01/2023
- Scripts for urgent public health matters where electronic prescribing would not be feasible

☐ Pharmacists are not required to verify if the script falls under one of the exceptions
  - If the written, oral, or faxed script is valid it may be filled without having to verify why it was not electronically prescribed

☐ An oral prescription issued by a practitioner may be communicated to a pharmacist by an expressly authorized employee or agent of the practitioner

☐ If an electronic prescription fails to transmit and is sent as a fax (failover), the pharmacist can fill it as if it's an oral prescription since it will contain all information except prescriber signature
  - For CVI medication only
  - Excluding Additional Drugs (IE: gabapentin)

☐ If an oral prescription is issued for a controlled substance in Schedule II-V under one of the exceptions discussed above (IE: emergency situation):
  - The amount prescribed can only be enough to cover through the emergency
  - The practitioner shall send:
    - An electronic prescription for the prescribed controlled substance within 2 days unless the practitioner has received a waiver from using an electronic prescription
    - The practitioner shall send a written prescription for the prescribed controlled substance to be delivered to the dispensing pharmacy within 7 days
      - If mailed, the follow-up prescription must be postmarked within the 7 business day timeframe
      - The follow-up prescription must include on its face a notation that the prescription is being issued "to document an oral prescription"
  - Persons charged with the enforcement of this chapter shall report violations to the board of registration in medicine, the

- board of registration in dentistry, the board of registration in podiatry or the board of registration in veterinary medicine, whichever is applicable, and to the commissioner or board of registration in pharmacy, whichever is applicable
- For CII only
  - The follow-up written or electronic prescription must include the additional notation, "Authorization for Emergency Dispensing"
  - If a prescriber fails to issue a follow-up written or electronic prescription within seven business days, the pharmacist is required to notify the U.S. Drug Enforcement Administration (DEA) of such failure
  - Must also notify the Commissioner of the Massachusetts Department of Public Health
- If a prescription is from an out-of-state prescriber for a CII-V, the registered pharmacist shall verify the prescription by telephone or other means. A pharmacist shall not fill a prescription for which said verification cannot be obtained
  - The pharmacist shall not be held liable for refusing to fill a prescription for which said verification cannot be obtained, provided that documented good faith efforts were made to determine the authenticity and validity of the prescription
- No prescription shall be issued in order for a practitioner to obtain controlled substances for supplying the practitioner for the purpose of general dispensing to patients
- To be valid, a prescription must be issued for a legitimate medical purpose by a practitioner in the usual course of his or her professional practice

- Prescription Must Include[6]
  - Name and address of prescriber
  - Registrant number of the practitioner (MCSR)
  - DEA number for CII-V
  - Date of issuance
  - Name, dosage, strength and quantity prescribed
  - Name and address of patient EXCEPT:
    - Veterinary script
    - Script for Naloxone or another opioid antagonist
    - Expedited Partner Therapy
  - Directions for use, including any cautionary statements
  - Number of refills
    - CII cannot be refilled
  - Must write "no substitution" for brand name only
    - On a written prescription, signing in a designated area is not valid, must use the "no substitution" language
  - Written prescriptions
    - Must be on tamper proof paper (adhering to Medicaid standards of security) unless transmitted via fax
      - Security features to prevent photocopying, modification of information, or use of counterfeit forms
    - Must have the provider's signature
  - Oral prescriptions
    - Name of authorized agent
    - The serial number assigned to the prescription by the dispensing pharmacy and the name of said pharmacy
  - CII opioid – prescribers must include a partial fill notation on all Schedule II opioid prescriptions. Prescribers may include this notation in writing or electronically
    - "Partial fill upon patient request"
    - A pharmacist receiving a prescription for a Schedule II opioid without the required notation must contact the prescriber or prescriber's authorized agent for confirmation and document the notation on the prescription in writing or electronically
    - Patient cannot be charged an extra co-pay for the partial fill
  - If written by mid-level provider, needs name of supervisor
  - Practitioners who wish to prescribe more than one Drug Product shall place each Prescription on a separate prescription
  - More than one Drug Product may be prescribed in the hospital setting on a single form or record provided, however, that the Prescription provides clear directions for use and interchange of each Drug Product

- Can NEVER be changed (all medication schedules):
  - Patient name (IE: changed to different patient)
  - Substance prescribed (except generic substitution if permitted)
  - Prescriber name
  - Prescriber signature
  - Earliest fill date (CII)
- Can be added or changed without consulting prescriber:
  - Patient address if omitted
  - Prescriber DEA if omitted
  - Day supply dispensed (only for drugs not reported to PMP)
    - IE: 30-day supply with 2 refills dispensed as one 90-day supply
    - Pharmacists are advised to exercise extreme caution with drug classes where a change in days supply may put a patient at risk
      - Narrow therapeutic index drugs (eg, lithium, warfarin) and behavioral health drugs (eg, antipsychotics, antidepressants) are two classes of drugs where changing the days supply may not be appropriate
- Can be changed with consultation:
  - NOTE: CII changes – must consult with prescriber
  - NOTE: CIII-VI – consult with prescriber or authorized agent
  - Date written can be added <u>only if omitted</u>
  - Prescriber address
  - Patient address change (if no address is on Rx, can add without consult but must consult if <u>changing</u> address - authorized agent or provider can do this for CII-VI)
  - Directions
  - Dosage form
  - Strength
  - Quantity prescribed
  - Supervisor physicians name for mid-level
  - Refills (CIII-VI)
  - No substitution language
- When changes made document: date, item changed/added, name of person authorizing change, name of pharmacist accepting change

- Needles and syringes[7]
    - Hypodermic syringes or hypodermic needles for the administration of controlled substances by injection may be sold in the commonwealth only by a pharmacist or wholesale druggist, a manufacturer of or dealer in surgical supplies or a manufacturer of or dealer in embalming supplies
    - No prescription needed

9 MASSACHUSETTS LAW – SCHEDULES, REFILLS, AND TRANSFERS

Medication Schedules[8]
- Schedules I-V follows federal guidelines
  - Hydrocodone-only extended release medication not in abuse deterrent form (CII) has special handling rules
    - Can only be handled by pharmacist or intern
      - NOT certified technician like other CII medications
    - Must be stored in securely locked cabinet within pharmacy
      - No option of dispersing with other drugs like other CII
    - Must be dispensed in childproof container or within a locked box
    - Prescriber must supply Letter of Medical Necessity for each prescription including diagnosis, treatment plan, and risk assessment
    - Must provide written warning with each prescription
    - Pharmacist must provide counseling
    - Pharmacist must check patient history on the Prescription Monitoring Program
  - Board regulations prohibit physicians, except in an emergency, from prescribing Schedule II controlled substances to a member of their immediate family
  - Physicians are prohibited from prescribing controlled substances in Schedules II through IV for their own use
- Schedule VI - all prescription medications not in Schedules I to V

- For the purposes of establishing criminal penalties for violation of a provision of this chapter, there are established the following five classes of controlled substances:
  - A, B, C, D, E
  - Violations involving Class A substances carry most severe punishments and violations involving Cass E substances have the least severe consequences
    - Class A examples
      - Gamma Hydroxy Butyric Acid
      - Heroine
      - Morphine
      - Fentanyl
      - Ketamine
    - Class B examples
      - Opium and opiate, and any salt, compound, derivative, or preparation of
      - MDMA
      - Methadone
      - LSD
      - Methylphenidate
      - Amphetamine
    - Class C examples
      - Benzodiazepines
      - Not more than 1.8 grams of codeine per 100 milliliters or not more than 90 milligrams per dosage unit with an equal or greater quantity of an isoquinoline alkaloid of opium
      - Mescaline
      - Peyote
      - Psilocybin
    - Class D examples
      - Phenobarbital
      - Marihuana
    - Class E examples
      - Not more than 200 milligrams of codeine per 100 milliliters or per 100 grams
      - Prescription drugs other than those included in Classes A, B, C, D

Refill Laws[9]

Schedule	Expiration	Refills/ Partial Fill Rules	Day Supply Limits
II	30 days	Partial fills within 30 days No refills	30 days* ** ***
II Nonnarcotic Out-of-state physician	5 days	Partial fills within 30 days No refills	30 days*
II Narcotic Physician from Connecticut, Rhode Island, New Hampshire, New York or Maine	5 days	Partial fills within 30 days No refills	30 days*
II Narcotic Physician from any other state	Pharmacy must be licensed in that state as well as Massachusetts	Partial fills within 30 days No refills	Must comply with MA and any other state laws
III	6 months	Maximum 5 refills	30 days* **
IV	6 months	Maximum 5 refills	Not specified
III, IV, V, VI Out-of-state prescriber	30 days	CIII-V 5 refills CVI not specified	CIII 30 days CIV-V Not specified
V	Not specified	Not specified	Not specified
VI	Not specified	Not specified	Not specified

*Exceptions for CII and III day supply limits: dextroamphetamine sulphate and methylphenidate hydrochloride may be filled for up to a 60 day supply if said substance is being used for the treatment of minimal brain dysfunction or narcolepsy, prescriptions for implantable infusion pumps consisting of Schedule II or Schedule III controlled substances may be filled for a maximum of 90 days

- The term "minimal brain dysfunction" means Attention Deficit/Hyperactivity Disorder (ADHD) or other accepted term for an inattention and impulsivity-hyperactivity disorder
- The term "dextro amphetamine sulfate" means a single entity drug product that contains the dextro and/or levo isomers of amphetamine and the salts thereof

** When issuing a prescription for an opiate to an adult patient for outpatient use for the first time, a practitioner shall not issue a prescription for more than a 7–day supply. A practitioner shall not issue an opiate prescription to a minor for more than a 7–day supply at any time and shall discuss with the parent or guardian of the minor the risks associated with opiate use and the reasons why the prescription is necessary. If, in the professional medical judgment of a practitioner, more than a 7–day supply of an opiate is required to treat the adult or minor patient's acute medical condition or is necessary for the treatment of chronic pain management, pain associated with a cancer diagnoses or for palliative care, then the practitioner may issue a prescription for the quantity needed to treat such acute medical condition, chronic pain, pain associated with a cancer diagnosis or pain experienced while the patient is in palliative care. The condition triggering the prescription of an opiate for more than a 7–day supply shall be documented in the patient's medical record and the practitioner shall indicate that a non-opiate alternative was not appropriate to address the medical condition

***Providers may issue multiple prescriptions totaling up to a 90-day supply of a CII medication utilizing "Do not fill before" language

- To prescribe methadone or buprenorphine for opioid addiction, prescriber needs authorization from Substance Abuse and Mental Health Services Administration (SAMHSA) and Massachusetts Bureau of Substance Abuse Services (BSAS)

- Out-of-State Prescriptions
    - Schedule III-VI prescriptions can be issued by any authorized practitioner from any state but must be filled within 30 days of the date written. Pharmacists must request and record that a written prescription be forwarded within seven days for any out-of-state Schedule III-V oral prescriptions
    - Nonnarcotic Schedule II prescriptions can only be issued by authorized <u>physicians</u> (no other practitioners) from any state
        - Must be filled within five days of the date written
    - Narcotic Schedule II prescriptions can only be issued by authorized <u>physicians</u> (no other practitioners) who are properly licensed and registered in Connecticut, Maine, Massachusetts, New Hampshire, New York, Rhode Island, or Vermont
        - Must be filled within five days of the date written
    - If a prescription is from an out-of-state prescriber for a CII-V, the registered pharmacist shall verify the prescription by telephone or other means
        - A pharmacist shall not fill a prescription for which said verification cannot be obtained. The pharmacist shall not be held liable for refusing to fill a prescription for which said

verification cannot be obtained, provided that documented good faith efforts were made to determine the authenticity and validity of the prescription
- In the case of any prescription for a Schedule II substance filled for an out-of-state provider, a pharmacist filling such prescription shall within thirty days after the filling of such prescription deliver to the department a copy of each such Schedule II prescription; provided, however, that such copy shall not include the name and address of the patient for whom the prescription is issued and that such copy and the information contained thereon shall not be deemed to be public record
- Transfers[10]
  - Must write the word "transfer" on incoming prescription
  - Must write the word "void" on face of outgoing invalidated prescription
  - All refills must be transferred
  - Record pharmacist and pharmacy name, DEA number
  - For CIII-V
    - May only be transferred once unless federal law says otherwise
  - For CVI
    - May only be transferred within 1 year of the date of issuance
  - Both original and transferred prescriptions must be maintained for 2 years from the date of last refill
  - Unfilled Electronic Prescriptions for Controlled Substances (EPCS) CII–V
    - May be transfer in accordance with the Drug Enforcement Administration (DEA)'s current rules or policies
  - Unfilled Paper, Fax or Oral Prescriptions for Controlled Substances CII–V
    - It is not permissible to transfer any original unfilled paper, fax or oral prescription for federally controlled substances
    - Entering an unfilled paper, fax or oral prescription into an electronic database does not transform the prescription into an EPCS. These prescriptions remain subject to all the regulations applicable to paper, fax, or oral prescriptions
    - After the original prescription is filled, the refills may be transferred
  - Unfilled or refill electronic, paper, fax or oral Schedule VI prescriptions may be transferred to another pharmacy

10 MASSACHUSETTS LAW – LABELING AND COUNCELLING

- Prescription labeling must contain[11]
    - Date of filling
    - Pharmacy name and address
    - Filling pharmacist's initials
    - Serial number of the prescription
    - Name of the patient, unless it is a veterinary prescription
    - Name of the prescribing practitioner
    - Name of the controlled substance
    - Directions for use
    - Cautionary statements, if any, contained in such prescription or required by law
    - If the controlled substance is dispensed as tablets or capsules the number in the container
    - For compounded medications
        - Label notifying prescribed users and practitioners that the drug is either a sterile or non-sterile compounded drug preparation
        - A telephone number to foster communication between patients in the commonwealth and a pharmacist employed by the pharmacy who has access to the patient's records. The phone shall be staffed during regular hours of operation every day and not less than 56 hours per week

- The department of public health shall produce and distribute either in written or electronic form to pharmacies, not including institutional pharmacies, pamphlets for consumers relative to narcotic drugs, specifically opiates, that includes educational information
    - A pharmacist shall distribute the pamphlet when dispensing a narcotic or controlled substance contained in Schedule II or III
- Counseling[12]
    - A pharmacist shall offer to counsel any person who presents a new prescription for filling. Such offer shall be made either by face to face communication between the pharmacist or the pharmacist's designee and the patient, or by telephone, except when the patient's needs or availability require an alternative method of counseling
    - If a person elects delivery of a prescription drug at a location other than a pharmacy, the requirements of this section may be satisfied by providing such person with access to a toll-free telephone service to facilitate communication between such person and the pharmacist at such pharmacy. The number of such toll-free telephone service shall be printed on a label affixed to each container of a prescription drug dispensed
        - Must offer a toll-free telephone number and must state the following:
            - "Dear patient, you have the right to know about the proper use of your medication and its effects. If you need more information please ask the pharmacist"
            - Printed material may accompany this statement provided the patient is informed it is not comprehensive and the patient should call if needed
    - Counseling can be made by the pharmacist or intern if supervised and must be available at all times the pharmacy is open
    - Nothing in this section shall be construed to require a pharmacist to provide counseling if the person presenting the prescription declines to accept such offer for counseling
    - The absence of any record of a failure to accept the pharmacist's offer to counsel shall create a presumption that such counseling was provided
    - These rules do not apply to inpatient medications or any setting where the medication is administered by an authorized individual

11 MASSACHUSETTS LAW – REGISTRANTS

License Expiration Reference Chart[13]

License	Expiration	Licensing Body	Reference
Pharmacist	December 31 even years	Board of Pharmacy	247 CMR 4.02
Pharmacy Technician	Biennially on birthday of licensee	Board of Pharmacy	M.G.L. c. 112 section 24C
Pharmacy (regular and controlled substance registration) including retail drug business within a retail food store or other retail store	December 31 uneven years	Board of Pharmacy	247 CMR 6.06, M.G.L. c. 112 section 39
Nuclear pharmacy	December 31 uneven years	Board of Pharmacy	M.G.L. c. 112 section 39B
Long-term care pharmacy or home infusion pharmacy	December 31 uneven years	Board of Pharmacy	M.G.L. c. 112 section 39C
Outsourcing facility (regular and controlled substance registration)	December 31 uneven year	Board of Pharmacy	M.G.L. c. 112 section 36E

License	Expiration	Licensing Body	Reference
Retail Sterile Pharmacy License*	Annually (IN ADDITION to regular pharmacy license)	Board of Pharmacy	M.G.L. c. 112 section 39G
Retail Complex Non-Sterile Compounding License*	Annually (IN ADDITION to regular pharmacy license)	Board of Pharmacy	M.G.L. c. 112 section 39H
Institutional Sterile Compounding Pharmacy*	Annually (IN ADDITION to regular pharmacy license)	Board of Pharmacy	M.G.L. c. 112 section 39I
Wholesale drug distributer (regular and controlled substance registration)	November 30 each year	Board of Pharmacy	M.G.L. c. 112 section 36B
Every person who manufactures, distributes or dispenses, or possesses any controlled substance**	1 year from the date of issuance***	Commissioner of Public Health (Controlled Substance Registration)	M.G.L. c. 94C section 7
Every person who is engaged in the analysis of controlled substances within a laboratory	1 year from the date of issuance	Commissioner of Public Health (Controlled Substance Registration)	M.G.L. c. 94C section 7
DEA registration	3 years	DEA	DEA Pharmacist's Manual

*Must have inspection; certify employees have been trained in lean concepts; disclose to the board the location, name and title of all principal managers and the name and Massachusetts license number of the designated manager of record

**Except in the case of a pharmacy, wholesale druggist or outsourcing facility whose controlled substance registration is via the Board of Pharmacy

***A separate registration shall be required at each principal place of business or professional practice where the registrant manufactures, distributes, or dispenses controlled substances (IE: registrations are location specific). If you plan to change name or address you need to apply for a new registration up to 90 days in advance

- Massachusetts law require every person who manufacturers, distributes, prescribes, administers, dispenses or possesses controlled substances in Schedules II-V to be registered with both the Department of Public Health (Massachusetts Controlled Substance Registration [MCSR]) and US Drug Enforcement Administration (DEA)
- Physicians, dentists, podiatrists, and veterinarians are automatically registered to dispense controlled substances and do not have to renew this registration
  - Must be registered with the DEA to dispense CII-V
- Massachusetts law recognizes all prescription drugs that are not federally scheduled (Schedule VI) as controlled substances
- Practitioners who only plan to manufacture, distribute, dispense, prescribe, administer, or possess Schedule VI drugs only need to get an MCSR (and not a DEA number)

- Besides providers, examples of those who must register include:
  - Municipalities or agencies
    - To possess medications for first responders to administer epinephrine, nerve agents, or opioid antagonists
      - Individuals need to be properly trained on these responsibilities
      - Should have healthcare provider overseeing if possible
  - Schools
    - To possess fluoride
  - Community programs
    - To assist in administration of prescriptions by non-self-administering individuals
    - Must be licensed provider or take training course every two years
    - Must be labeled properly and stored in a securely locked area
    - Must document administration and keep medication references on hand
    - Must be written protocols and procedures in place

- The following persons shall not require registration and may lawfully possess and distribute controlled substances:
  - An agent or employee of any manufacturer, distributor, or dispenser registered under this chapter, if he is acting in the usual course of his business or employment
    - A salesman or other field representative of a registered manufacturer, wholesaler, jobber or dealer in controlled substances may not possess any controlled substance in schedule I-V for the purpose of demonstrating, displaying, selling, or distributing as samples
  - A common or contract carrier or warehouseman, or an employee thereof, whose possession of any controlled substance is in the usual course of business or employment
  - Any public official or law enforcement officer acting in the regular performance of his official duties
  - A registered nurse or licensed practical nurse or a licensed dental hygienist under the supervision of a practitioner in the course of their professional practice
  - Any therapist, technician, or medical student when performing under the supervision of a practitioner those services which are defined to be functions of their respective callings
  - An ultimate user or research subject may lawfully possess or administer a controlled substance at the direction of a practitioner
  - No person shall be required to register for the purpose of purchasing, storing, possessing, or administering naloxone or other opioid antagonists
- Notwithstanding any other provision of this section, the commissioner shall, upon receipt of the fee, automatically issue to any physician, dentist, podiatrist or veterinarian who is authorized to practice in the commonwealth a registration to dispense
- A provider may possess controlled substances as may reasonably be required for the purpose of patient treatment and may administer controlled substances or may cause the same to be administered under his direction by a nurse
  - Physician may dispense by delivering to an ultimate user a controlled substance in CII-V a single dose or in a quantity that is essential for the treatment of a patient
    - The amount or quantity of any controlled substance dispensed under this subsection shall not exceed the quantity of a controlled substance necessary for the immediate and proper treatment of the patient until it is possible for the patient to have a prescription filled by a pharmacy

- Mid-level practitioners cannot possess CII-V for patient dispensing
- For opioid addiction, while arranging for care, a prescriber can administer 1 day of medications at a time for a maximum of 3 days
- Physicians who stock CII-III must maintain records of:
  - Receipt of substances
  - Name and address of patient to whom it was dispensed or administered
  - Name, dosage, strength of each substance
  - Date of administering or dispensing
- Must inventory CII-V every 2 years and keep records for 2 years after inventory
  - CII must be separate from CIII-V
- CII-V must be stored in a locked cabinet in office

□ For samples of medications in CVI
- A maximum of a 30-day supply can be dispensed by practitioner
- 90-day supply may be dispensed only as part of an indigent patient program

□ Must record:
- The name, dosage and strength of the substance dispensed
- The volume of units dispensed
- The date of the dispensing
- The name and address of the person to whom the medication was dispensed

□ Samples must be properly labeled with:
- Practitioner's name and address
- Date of dispensing
- Name of patient
- Name, dosage form, and strength of medication
- Directions for use and any necessary cautionary statements
- Expiration date

- Revocation, Suspension, Refusal to Renew
  - Summary Cease and Desist Notice (Summary Suspension)
    - The board of registration in pharmacy in the case of a retail drug business, wholesale druggist or outsourcing facility or the commissioner in all other cases may <u>without hearing</u> suspend or refuse to renew any registration if he finds that there is an imminent danger to the public health or safety
  - Summary Quarantine Notice
    - Suspension <u>prior to a hearing</u> to prevent the use of medications prepared by a registrant to protect the public health, safety, or welfare
  - Grounds for revocation, suspension, or refusal to renew a registration include, but are not limited to, whether the registrant:
    - Has furnished false or fraudulent material information in any application filed under the provisions of 105 CMR 700.000
    - Has been convicted under any state or federal law of any criminal violation relating to his or her fitness to be registered under 105 CMR 700.000
    - Has had his or her federal registration suspended or revoked to manufacture, distribute, dispense, administer or possess controlled substances
    - Is found to be unfit or unqualified to manufacture, distribute, dispense, or possess any controlled substance
    - Has violated any provision of M.G.L. c. 94C
    - Has used the online prescription monitoring program system, or prescription data derived therefrom, in a manner inconsistent with the terms and conditions for such use

- Pharmacists
  - Applicant must pass Multistate Pharmacy Jurisprudence Examination (MPJE) and North American Pharmacist Licensure Examination (NAPLEX) within a 1-year period or must retake both
- Pharmacist License – Expired or Suspended[14]

Time Frame	Late Fee	Additional CE	Written Petition	MPJE	NAPLEX	Internship Hours
≤60 days (NOT suspended or revoked)	Yes	X	X	X	X	X
60 days to 2 years (NOT suspended or revoked)	Yes	If BOP wants	X	X	X	X
>2 years (NOT suspended or revoked)	Yes	Yes	Yes	Yes	If the person has not been practicing in another state and the BOP wants	If the person has not been practicing and the BOP wants
Suspended or revoked for 6 months to 2 years	-	-	Yes	Yes	If BOP wants	If BOP wants
Suspended or revoked for >2 years	-	-	Yes	Yes	If BOP wants	If BOP wants

- Pharmacist Continuing Education (CE)[15]

Category	Number of CEs (per year unless otherwise specified)
Total Per Calendar Year	20
Max Contact Hours in 1 day	8
Live Contact Hours	5
Pharmacy Law	2
Immunization	1 every 2 years
Collaborative Practice Agreement	5 additional hours (IE: total of 25 CE per year)
Sterile Compounding (if applicable)	5 (note: counts towards 20)
Complex Non-Sterile Compounding (if applicable)	3 (note: counts towards 20)

- If licensed on or after October 1, pharmacist has until April 30 of next year to get CEs done
- No CEs needed during year a pharmacist graduates from pharmacy school

- Registration Types[16]

	Technician Trainee	Technician	Certified Technician	Intern
May relay pharmacist's offer to counsel	Yes	Yes	Yes	Yes
May compound sterile and non-sterile medications	Yes	Yes	Yes	Yes
May reconstitute medications	Yes	Yes	Yes	Yes
May conduct remote processing of prescriptions in accordance with the shared services policy	X	Yes	Yes	Yes
May assist in the transport of CII drugs	X	Yes	Yes	Yes
May assist in the handling of CII drugs	X	X	Yes	Yes
May handle hydrocodone-only extended release medication in a non-abuse deterrent form	X	X	X	Yes
May take refill prescriptions over the phone	X	Yes	Yes	Yes
May take new prescriptions over the phone	X	X	Yes	Yes
May perform prescription transfers of CVI drugs	X	X	Yes	Yes
May stock and return prescriptions from Automated Pharmacy System	X	X	Yes	Yes
May load Automated Dispensing Device (ADD)***	X	X	Yes	Yes
May contact prescriber concerning therapy clarifications or modifications	X	X	X	Yes*
May administer vaccines	X	X**	X**	Yes*
May do all pharmacist duties if properly supervised	X	X	X	Yes*

*Under direct pharmacist supervision
**Note there are some provisions for technicians to administer vaccines for COVID-19 however this is temporary
*** If the ADD is only to be used for emergency medication kits or hospice kits, it may be loaded by a certified pharmacy technician, pharmacy intern, pharmacist, or licensed nurse

- Pharmacy Technician Trainee (PTT)
  - 16 years of age or older
  - May not work for >1500 hours or >1 year, whichever is shorter, unless:
    - Board grants an extension
    - Individual is not 18 years old yet
    - Individual has not completed at least 500 hours of employment
- Pharmacy Technician (PT)
  - 18 years of age or older
  - Must pass Board-approved pharmacy technician assessment examination after completing a technician training program or working 500 hours as a trainee
  - If applicant possesses a pharmacy technician license in another state the board may accept this instead if license is in good standing
- Certified Pharmacy Technician (CPhT)
  - Certified by a Board-approved certifying body
  - If certification lapses, may function as PT until current
- Intern
  - Must be in the professional years of pharmacy school or graduate obtaining hours until licensure
  - Needs direct supervision by a Board-approved pharmacist preceptor
    - Preceptor is a registered pharmacist in good standing, who has completed at least one year of the actual practice of Pharmacy; must also be approved by the Board to supervise and direct the training of pharmacy interns
  - May engage in the full range of activities conducted by a registered pharmacist provided direct supervision of a registered pharmacist preceptor at all times
    - Including immunizations if the intern has completed an immunization training program
  - Must notify BOP within 14 days if withdraw from school
- Supervision Rules
  - Pharmacists can supervise a maximum of 4 support personnel
    - Maximum of two PTT or PT
    - Two pharmacy interns maximum
      - Exceptions for internal medicine APPE students or when conducting immunization clinics, max 4 interns
  - Sales clerks, messengers, delivery personnel are not included

- Licensed pharmacy staff who are assigned to train other pharmacy support staff are not required to be included in the supervisory ratios as long as such persons are not independently supporting the pharmacist in any professional capacity and are appropriately designated on the published schedule
  - Trainer must oversee the trainee at all times
  - A trainee who is doing exclusively computer-based training modules does not need supervision and need not be counted towards the supervisory ratio as long as that "Trainee" is scheduled for computer training for a specified amount of time and does not engage in any activities that support the pharmacist in any professional capacity

12 MASSACHUSETTS LAW – PHARMACY OPERATIONS

- Pharmacy Operations During the Temporary Absence of a Pharmacist[17]
  - In any pharmacy that is staffed by a single pharmacist, the pharmacist may leave the pharmacy temporarily for necessary and appropriate breaks and meal periods without closing the pharmacy and removing ancillary staff from the pharmacy if the pharmacist reasonably believes that the security of the dangerous drugs and devices will be maintained in his or her absence
    - The break shall not exceed 30 minutes
    - The pharmacist must remain on premise
  - Can sell medications during absence if:
    - The prescription medication is a refill medication that the pharmacist has checked and determined not to require the consultation of a pharmacist
    - A new prescription which has been previously prepared, visibly checked by a pharmacist and had a drug utilization performed by a pharmacist, may be picked up by a patient provided that a log, including the patients phone number, of all such transactions is kept
      - ✓ The pharmacist, upon return from break, and within a reasonable time, shall call the patient to review any pertinent counseling deemed appropriate

- Pharmacy Requirements[18]
  - Pharmacy registration must be signed by the pharmacist who will oversee the pharmacy
  - A pharmacy cannot be owned by a practitioner with prescriptive privileges
  - Must maintain on premise:
    - A current copy or electronic version of the Massachusetts List of Interchangeable Drugs (MLID), including the Orange Book, Additional List, Exception List
    - A current copy or electronic version (with quarterly updates) of a compendia appropriate to the practice setting approved by the pharmacist manager of record
    - A current copy or electronic version of the Board Regulations (247 CMR)
    - A balance capable of accurately weighing quantities as small as 13 mg
      - ✓ Balance shall be tested and sealed by the state or local sealer of weights and measures annually
    - The equipment necessary to conduct the practice of pharmacy according to the standards set forth by most current edition of the United States Pharmacopoeia
    - Prescription labels which bear the name and address of the proposed pharmacy
    - Appropriate sanitary appliances, including a suitable sink which shall be equipped for hot and cold running water and which shall be situated in or near the area in which prescriptions are to be filled
    - Whenever applicable, at least one bound book for recording sales of controlled substances which may be sold over-the-counter without a prescription
    - Whenever applicable, at least one book for recording sales of alcoholic beverages and signatures of the purchasers of these beverages
    - A prescription area of not less than 300 square feet to accommodate the appropriate pharmaceutical equipment, apparatus, and supplies, and to facilitate the proper preparation and compounding of prescribed medications
    - If the pharmacy does sterile compounding:
      - ✓ Clean room of at least 72 square feet
      - ✓ Closed on all sides except door and pass through
      - ✓ Must get board approval and this approval must be conspicuously posted and visible to the public

- "Patient Consultation Area" that provides adequate privacy
  - Must be accessible without having to walk through stockroom or dispensing area
- A pharmacy registered in the commonwealth to dispense CII-V drugs shall make available prescription lock boxes for sale at each store location
  - Pharmacies shall make customers aware of the availability of the lock boxes by displaying a sign on or near the pharmacy counter that is at least 4 inches by 5 inches and includes the following statement in legibly printed font: "Lock boxes for securing your prescription medications are available at this pharmacy"[19]
- Reasonably-sized sign on main entrance identifying presence of a pharmacy or pharmacy department
  - Name of the pharmacist Manager of Record must be displayed on or adjacent to the main entrance
  - Hours of operation shall be prominently posted at all consumer entrances
- Pharmacy permit
- Massachusetts Controlled Substance Registration
- DEA Controlled Substance Registration
- Certificate of Fitness (if applicable)
- A sign of not less than 11 by 14 inches in a conspicuous place stating:
  - "Dear patients, you have the right to know about the proper use of your medication and its effects. If you need more information please ask the pharmacist"
- Each pharmacist who is a full-time employee shall have readily available or displayed in a conspicuous place his or her certificate of registration and the original or a copy of his or her current wallet registration
- Refrigerator and freezer
  - Assure that cold chain (temperature-controlled supply chain) processes are maintained at all times
  - Refrigerator: between 36°F to 46°F (2°C to 8°C)
  - Freezer: between -13°F and 14°F (-25°C and -10°C)
  - Develop a policy and procedure to handle the maintenance, monitoring, and cleaning of the equipment
    - Establish a back-up plan to assure proper storage of refrigerated or frozen medications in the event of a power failure or other unforeseen event

- ✓ Review and document temperatures of each unit at least twice daily
  - On any days the pharmacy may be closed, the pharmacy must have a mechanism in place to identify any temperature excursions
  - Each temperature log must identify the corresponding refrigerator or freezer unit, identify the reviewer (e.g. name or initials), and be readily retrievable
- ✓ Can NOT store food or beverage products in refrigerators or freezers used for medications
- Manager of Record (MOR)
  - Can only be Manager of Record for one pharmacy at a time
  - Whenever there is a change in Manager of Record, you must take a complete inventory of all controls CII-V
    - ✓ Should be signed by new MOR and outgoing MOR unless outgoing MOR is unavailable due to death, serious injury, or termination due to inappropriate handling of controlled substances in which case staff pharmacist may sign
      - Must notify Board why the staff pharmacist is signing
    - ✓ Do not send inventory to the board in most circumstances but send sworn statement that it has been taken
  - Must notify Board within 10 working days of any change in MOR
  - If MOR will be absent from the pharmacy for >30 and <100 days, an interim MOR must be named and an inventory of controlled substances must be taken
  - If MOR will be absent from the pharmacy for >100 days a new MOR must be named and change of MOR procedures are followed
  - Responsibilities of MOR include:
    - ✓ Maintaining reference texts, records, security
    - ✓ Establishing and enforcing policies and procedures
    - ✓ Maintaining adequate staff
    - ✓ Biennial inventory
- Certificate of Fitness
  - Allows sale of alcohol and to use alcohol to make medicinal preparations
    - ✓ Cannot sell alcohol on Sundays or holidays except by prescription

- Bound record book
  - Date of sale, name and address of purchaser, kind, quantity, price
  - Must sign and date statement: "I wish to purchase (name of alcoholic beverage). I certify that I am of statutory age to purchase alcoholic beverages and that the alcoholic beverage is to be used for mechanical, chemical, medicinal purpose" (select one)
- Closing a Pharmacy[20]
  - Must notify the board in writing using certified mail at least 14 days before the intended closing
    - Verify that adequate advance notice has been given to customers
    - Outline the intended closing procedures and how you will dispose of or transfer controlled substances
      - If you are transferring controlled substances, you must notify the BOP by certified mail at least 14 days in advance
        - Provide information including:
          - (i) Name, address, phone number of both parties
          - (ii) Pharmacy permit numbers
          - (iii) Pharmacy controlled substance registration numbers
          - (iv) Name and pharmacist registration numbers of Managers of Record
          - (v) Date on which transfer will take place
        - On date of transfer take a complete inventory of all CII-V signed by both Managers of Record
        - Both parties must keep a copy of inventory for 2 years
        - A copy of the inventory must be filed with the board within 10 days of the transfer
  - Within 10 days of the closure, you must:
    - Return pharmacy permit to the board
    - Return controlled substance registration to the board
    - Return Certificate of Fitness to the board if applicable
    - Notify BOP that all controlled substances have been properly disposed of or transferred

13 MASSACHUSETTS LAW – MISC. PHARMACY TYPES

- Hospitals, Long Term Care Facilities (LTCF), Hospice[21]
    - Hospital pharmacies may fill medication orders for hospital inpatients, prescriptions for hospital outpatients and employees, and medication orders or prescriptions for inpatients of a hospital-based skilled nursing facility or a long-term care facility that is solely owned by a hospital. Patients of such a hospital-based skilled nursing facility or long-term care facility shall be considered hospital patients for the purposes of receiving pharmacy services
    - Hospital pharmacies and their satellites or branches may fill prescriptions for emergency room patients and discharge patients in an amount not to exceed a 14-day supply of the prescribed medication

- LTCF Emergency Kits[22]
    - Maximum Dosage Units (individually packaged single dose form)

	<50 beds	51-100	101-150	>150
Analgesics CII-V	45	60	75	90
Sedatives/Anticonvulsants CII-V	15	20	25	30

- LTCF should develop its own formulary in conjunction with a pharmacy provider
- Automated dispensing machines are permitted rather than emergency lock boxes

- Hospice Acute Meds[23]
  - Non-patient specific medications stored on-site at hospice facility – only to be used to treat the patient until the pharmacy can fill and deliver the full prescription
  - The pharmacy provider must utilize an Automated Dispensing Device (ADD) to store and secure acute use medications as well as obtain a machine-specific Controlled Substance Registration (CSR) from the Board of Registration in Pharmacy. The pharmacy provider must also determine whether a machine-specific DEA number is required
    - The pharmacy must reconcile all medications dispensed through the ADD with prescriptions
    - The contents of the ADD, until dispensed for administration pursuant to a prescriber's prescription or order, remain the property of the pharmacy
  - Maximum Dosage Units (individually packaged single dose form)

	≤ 10 beds	11-20 beds	≥ 21 beds
Analgesics CII-V	50	100	150
Sedatives/Anticonvulsants CII-V	30	60	90
CVI	25	50	75

- Nuclear Pharmacies[24]
  - Must maintain on premise:
    - Most recent edition of United States Pharmacopoeia
    - Most recent edition of Remington's Pharmaceutical Sciences
    - Current texts on the practice of nuclear pharmacy and radiation safety
    - Dose preparation station
    - Dose caliber
    - Exhaust hood and filter system
    - Refrigerator exclusively for radioactive materials
    - Chromatographic apparatus
    - Portable radiation survey meter
    - Area radiation detection room monitors
    - Personnel dosimeters
    - Scintillation analyzer
    - Dispensing supplies
  - No entrances or exits shall connect directly with other places of business
  - At least one qualified nuclear pharmacist shall be in personal attendance at the pharmacy at all times

- Must keep records of acquisition and disposition of all radiopharmaceuticals for at least 3 years
- If the name of the patient is unknown at the time a prescription is received, the nuclear pharmacy shall obtain the patient's name and address (or address of facility) with 72 hours after dispensing
- Outer container labeling must state:
  - Radiation symbol and words "Caution Radioactive Material"
  - Name of the radionucleotide
  - Amount of radioactive material
  - Warning labels if needed
  - Expiration date and/or time
- Nuclear pharmacists must be registered and approved of by the Board of Pharmacy
  - 200 contact hours of formal academic training in radiopharmaceuticals with no more than 60 of said hours being acquired through laboratory training
  - Minimum of 3 months full time or 500 hours of actual on the job training

- Outsourcing Facility[25]
  - To register with the Board of Pharmacy as an outsourcing facility you must:
    - Be registered with the FDA as a 503B
    - Have proof of an FDA inspection within 2 years immediately preceding the application
      - ✓ An instate facility may be granted a provisional license if the facility has not been inspected in >2 years
        - They may compound but cannot dispense sterile compounds until inspected and receive full registration

14 MASSACHUSETTS LAW – STANDING ORDERS

- Standing Orders and Pharmacist Administration[26]
    - Emergency Contraceptives
        - Copy of Standing Order must be filed with SBOP
        - Standing order and proof of pharmacist training must be readily retrievable at the pharmacy
        - Must report total number of Emergency Contraceptives dispensed pursuant to Standing Order annually by August 1 for time frame July 1 to June 30
    - Naloxone
        - A pharmacy may dispense naloxone either pursuant to a patient-specific prescription or the statewide standing order
            - Statewide standing order is for 2 doses of intranasal or intramuscular naloxone
        - There is no limit to the amount of naloxone that may be dispensed to an individual. Massachusetts state law specifically allows for an individual to obtain naloxone with the intention to administer it to another person
        - Unless the purchaser requests otherwise, the pharmacy must make a reasonable effort to determine if the purchaser's insurance covers naloxone
        - Naloxone rescue kits must be labeled with the expiration date of the included naloxone unit
        - In place of the name and address, "Naloxone Rescue Kit," may be used to create a patient profile and prescription label

- Annually, by January 15th, each pharmacy must submit a report via email including the following information for the previous calendar year:
  - The name and zip code of the pharmacy
  - The total number of naloxone doses (not prescriptions or manufacturer-supplied units) dispensed
  - The total number of those doses paid for with insurance
- The board of registration in pharmacy shall promulgate regulations requiring pharmacies located in areas with high incidents of opiate overdose, as determined by the board in consultation with the department of public health, to maintain a continuous supply of naloxone rescue kits or opioid antagonist medications
  - A person who, in good faith, seeks medical assistance for someone experiencing a drug-related overdose shall not be charged or prosecuted for possession of a controlled substance[27]

- Immunizations
  - A registered pharmacist and pharmacist intern may dispense by administration vaccinations to persons nine years of age or older
  - Standing order can be for any CDC recommended vaccines
  - Proof of immunizer training course must be kept on premise
  - Board-licensed pharmacies may conduct off-site immunization clinics utilizing qualified pharmacy personnel as long as a Massachusetts licensed pharmacist is present
- Medications for the Treatment of Mental Illness and Substance Use Disorder
  - A pharmacist or a pharmacy intern may administer FDA-approved mental health and substance use disorder treatment drugs to persons 18 years or older provided that:
    - Administration is conducted pursuant to a valid prescription
    - The pharmacist or pharmacy intern does not administer the first dose of such medication the person receives
    - The prescription is subject to reassessment by the prescriber at appropriate intervals, as determined by the prescriber (IE: quarterly)
    - Training accredited by the Centers for Disease Control and Prevention, the American Council on Pharmaceutical Education or a similar health authority or professional body appropriate for the medications being administered and their respective patient population

- ✓ A pharmacist or pharmacy intern must maintain current certification in cardiopulmonary resuscitation
- ✓ A pharmacist or pharmacy intern must provide customary, patient counseling prior to administering a dose of an approved medication
- ✓ A pharmacy where any of the eligible medications are administered must maintain the following information:
    - Patient consent
    - Patient screening information, including at least date of birth and other relevant vital statistics, known allergies, and other medications taken
    - Type of medication administered
    - Manufacturer
    - Lot number
    - Expiration date
    - Date of administration
    - Route and site of administration
    - Pharmacist or pharmacy intern (signature or initials and title) administering
    - Adverse outcome, if any
    - Adverse event, if any
- ✓ Any adverse events or reactions occurring as a result of a pharmacist or pharmacy intern administering a medication listed in this guidance should be appropriately communicated to the prescriber within 24 hours. If the adverse event is serious, the event must be immediately reported to the prescriber

▲ Long Acting Injectable Antipsychotics (LAIs)
- ✓ Aripiprazole (Abilify Maintena®)
- ✓ Aripiprazole lauroxil (Aristada®)
- ✓ Fluphenazine decanoate (Prolixin decanoate®)
- ✓ Haloperidol decanoate (Haldol decanoate®)
- ✓ Paliperidone palmitate (Invega Sustenna®)
- ✓ Paliperidone palmitate (Invega Trinza®)
- ✓ Risperidone (Risperdal Consta®)
- ✓ Risperidone ER (Perseris®)

▲ Long Acting Injectable Medication for Substance Use Disorders
- ✓ Naltrexone (Vivitrol®)

15 MASSACHUSETTS LAW – THEFT AND LOSS

- Reporting Theft or Loss[28]
  - Must report to DEA:
    - Theft or significant loss
      - You determine if a loss is significant based on your business
    - Pharmacy must notify in writing the local DEA Diversion Field Office within one business day of discovery of a theft or significant loss of a controlled substance (CI-V)
    - A pharmacy must also complete a DEA Form 106 (Report of Theft or Loss of Controlled Substances)
    - If, after the initial notification to DEA, the investigation of the theft or loss determines no such theft or loss of controlled substances occurred, a DEA Form 106 does not need to be filed. However, the registrant must notify DEA in writing of this fact in order to resolve the initial report and explain why no DEA Form 106 was filed regarding the incident
  - Must report to police:
    - Simultaneously when you report to DEA you must send DEA Form 106 to the state police for a distributer or to the town and state police for a dispenser
  - Must report to Commissioner (for providers who dispense):
    - Within 24 hours of discovery of such theft or loss
  - Must report to Board of Pharmacy:
    - All losses related to employee stealing/diversion, in any schedule or quantity
    - "Significant" loss of CII-V
    - "Significant" loss of CVI that is additional drug for MassPAT (IE: gabapentin)

- Submit information to BOP via email within seven business days of the discovery of a possible significant loss including the following information:
  - Pharmacy Name
  - Pharmacy State License Number
  - Pharmacy Address (including city/town & zip code)
  - Manager of Record Name
  - Date of Possible Loss
  - Drug name(s), strength, and dosage form
  - Reason for Possible Loss, if known
- Within the next 21 days, or upon completion of investigation, whichever comes first, the pharmacy must then report to the Board the findings of its investigation
  - Outcome can be significant loss, no loss, or loss that is not reportable
  - Regardless of the outcome of the investigation, the pharmacy must submit the outcome of its investigation
- If the investigation confirms a significant loss, the report must be submitted within seven business days of confirming a significant loss:
  - The Board's Report of Loss of Controlled Substances form
  - DEA Form 106, if applicable
  - Other required documents
    - For EACH THEFT OR SIGNIFICANT LOSS, provide a statement that includes the following:
      (i) The manner in which the loss was discovered and the date of discovery
      (ii) A description as to how the loss occurred and the reason why such may have occurred
      (iii) A description of the security cameras in the pharmacy, where they are located, if footage was viewed and what the footage revealed. If footage was not reviewed, state the reason it was not reviewed. State the time period security videos are saved and/or archived
      (iv) Any corrective actions taken by the pharmacy, including, but not limited to, disciplinary actions, process improvements, and changes to policies and procedures

- (v) Contact information, including email addresses, of the manager of record and any involved loss prevention personnel
- For EACH THEFT OR SIGNIFICANT LOSS, submit the following materials:
  - (i) The pharmacy's internal investigation, including incident reports, loss prevention reports, employee statements, and witnesses statements
  - (ii) Police report (if applicable)
  - (iii) Reconciliation report(s) for the lost medication(s)
  - (iv) Interview statements of employees and witnesses regarding the loss
  - (v) Copy of relevant security footage
- For each theft or significant loss of a SCHEDULE II controlled substance:
  - (i) Submit all information plus:
    1. Submit an attestation confirming reconciliation of the perpetual inventory for all Schedule II controlled substances are conducted by a pharmacist at least every 10 days. If they are not conducted at least every 10 days, please indicate why
    2. Reconcile DEA 222 forms and purchase invoices against the perpetual inventory for the 3 months prior to the loss until the present date
       a. Include a signed statement that describes if the reconciliation revealed any further discrepancies and describe the nature of the discrepancies and follow up
- If the DEA 106 Form indicates the TYPE OF LOSS is "OTHER," the pharmacy MUST submit a report that includes the following:
  - (i) An attestation confirming the pharmacy reviewed perpetual inventories, cycle counts, biennial inventory, and inventory reports for the time period to include at least 3 months prior to the loss, as well as a description of the inventory review undertaken. The description shall identify any periods of non-compliance with inventory requirements. The description shall identify any discrepancies

- (ii) An attestation confirming the pharmacy reviewed all staffing schedules and identified all staff that had access to the pharmacy at the time of the loss, including any floating or temporary staff
- (iii) A statement describing any changes in operations, policies, or procedures at the time of the loss
- (iv) A statement of the loss as a percentage of total number of units (IE: tablets, milliliters, etc.) of that specific medication and strength dispensed by the pharmacy per month
- (v) A listing of all corporate and/or store policies pertaining to controlled substance ordering, receiving, accountability, and management along with a statement describing whether policies and procedures were followed. If proper policies and procedures were not followed, provide a detailed response explaining the breakdown including the name and license number of each individual involved
- Upon completion of the investigation, if it is determined that no significant loss of controlled substances occurred, provide a statement that includes the following:
  - (i) A detailed description of the investigatory process which concluded there was no loss, no significant loss of medication(s), OR how the pharmacy can otherwise account for the medication(s) in the initial notification
- If it is determined that a significant loss did not occur, the pharmacy must report back to the Board with a detailed description of the investigatory process that concluded no reportable loss occurred
  - ✓ Non reportable losses include insignificant losses and losses resulting from confirmed dispensing errors

- Quality Related Events (QRE)[29]
  - Incorrect dispensing of a prescribed medication including failure to recognize drug utilization issues
  - Continuous Quality Improvement (CQI) Program
    - Program to detect, document, assess and prevent QREs
    - Analyze data from QREs
    - Provide ongoing education at least annually to pharmacy personnel
  - Upon discovery of a QRE, pharmacy personnel should report immediately to pharmacist on duty or pharmacy manager. This pharmacist must:
    - Notify patient
    - Notify prescriber if they feel necessary
    - Provide directions for correcting the error
    - Provide instructions for minimizing negative impact on the patient
  - Must document QRE on the day discovered
    - Document how error discovered, description of error
    - Document contact with patient and prescriber
  - QRE analysis
    - Recommended changes to procedures, systems, processes, etc.
  - Must maintain a record of all QREs for 2 years from the date of the QRE report
  - Must report to BOP any improper dispensing that causes serious injury or death within 15 business days of the pharmacy discovering or being informed

16 MASSACHUSETTS LAW – COMPOUNDING

- Compounding, including veterinary compounding, must[30]
    - Be pursuant to a patient specific prescription or in anticipation of a patient specific prescription based on routine, regularly-observed prescribing patterns
    - Meet the unique medical need of an individual patient by producing a significant difference between the compounded drug preparation and a comparable commercially available drug
    - Be accompanied by a documented medical need for the compounded preparation. Reasons may include the removal of a dye, change in strength, change in dosage, form or delivery mechanism
        - Please note that a price difference between a compounded preparation and commercially available product is not a significant difference to justify compounding
    - The Board plans to follow the FDA's guidance on what may be compounded

- Sterile Compounding Responses[31]
    - All sterile compounding pharmacies licensed by the Board must report, respond to, and properly remediate above action level environmental monitoring (EM) results in ISO classified spaces
    - This policy pertains to any Massachusetts licensed pharmacy that compounds sterile preparations to be dispensed into or from the Commonwealth

- Above Action Level Environmental Monitoring Results are defined as EM results of non-viable air and viable air and surface samples meeting or exceeding the criteria as outlined below:

	Non-Viable Particles ≥ 0.5 um	Viable Air Samples	Surface Samples
ISO Class 5	> 3,520 particles/m^3	>1 CFU	>3 CFU
ISO Class 7	> 352,000 particles/m^3	>10 CFU	>5 CFU
ISO Class 8	> 3,520,000 particles/m^3	>100 CFU	>50 CFU

- CFU = colony-forming unit
- ≥ 1 CFU of highly pathologic microorganisms including gram negative rods, coagulase positive staphylococcus and fungi for any ISO level

  - Upon notification of above action level EM results, a pharmacy must immediately assess and investigate above action level EM results and must not prepare any compounded sterile products (CSPs) until a remediation plan of the affected area(s) is initiated
  - >15 CFU in an ISO Class 5 environment triggers significant loss of control and you must:
    - Recall any CSPs that are within their beyond use dates
    - Perform adverse event surveillance
    - Contact prescriber(s)
    - Engage a microbiologist, industrial hygienist, or infection control professional
  - A pharmacy with a repeat above action level EM result (consecutive or non-consecutive) for the same ISO-classified area occurring within 60 days must engage a microbiologist, industrial hygienist, or infection control professional
  - Within 7 days of notification of result, a signed copy of Disclosure of Above Action Level Environmental Monitoring (EM) Results Form 1: Initial Reporting Form and EM report must be scanned and emailed to: abnormalresults@MassMail.State.MA.US
    - Specify the name of the pharmacy, town, and state in the subject line
  - Within 21 days of Initial Reporting Form submission, the final repeat EM report must be submitted using Form 2: Final Reporting Form

- Remediation Process
  - Root Cause Analysis (RCA)
    - A pharmacy must conduct an investigation into the root cause of any above action level EM result or adverse trend in environmental monitoring
  - Repeat Environmental Monitoring
    - A pharmacy must demonstrate successful remediation by performing repeat EM of air and surfaces
      - The pharmacy may limit the repeat EM to the affected ISO classified space based on the pharmacy's EM sampling plan unless otherwise directed by the Board
      - All sample locations in the affected ISO classified space must be resampled
    - If the repeat EM falls within the action levels of this policy, the pharmacy may resume its standard BUDs or resume compounding, as applicable
  - Corrective Action and Preventative Action (CAPA) Plan must, at a minimum, include:
    - Documentation of actions taken as result of the investigation into the RCA (IE: triple clean, retraining, increased EM monitoring, etc.)
    - Repeat EM (resampling) and microbiology report review
- During remediation process, pharmacy can compound if they have performed remediation steps and done a risk assessment
- BUDs during Remediation Process

Failure Environment	Room Temperature	Refrigerated
ISO Class 5	Immediate Use*	N/A
ISO Class 7	24 hours	3 days
ISO Class 8	24 hours (if starting from nonsterile ingredients)	3 days (if starting from nonsterile ingredients)
	30 hours (if starting from sterile ingredients)	9 days (if starting from sterile ingredients)

*A pharmacy shall not resume compounding in an ISO Class 5 primary engineering control following an above action level EM result until remediation is complete and repeat EM results are proven acceptable

- If the pharmacy has multiple PEC then the pharmacy can continue to compound in the unaffected PECs if the pharmacy's risk assessment deems appropriate
- If the pharmacy only has 1 PEC, any CSPs compounded must follow the immediate use requirements

- Types of Non-Sterile Compounds[32]
  - Simple non-sterile compounding
    - Making a preparation that:
      - Is the subject of a United States Pharmacopeia (USP) compounding monograph; or
      - Appears in a peer-reviewed journal article that contains specific quantities of all components, compounding procedure and equipment, and stability data for that formulation with appropriate BUDs (USP <795>)
    - Examples of simple non-sterile compounding include:
      - Allopurinol oral suspension
      - Captopril oral solution
      - Ursodiol oral suspension
      - Coal tar ointment
      - Some commercially manufactured prescription compounding kits (IE: vancomycin compounding kit)
  - Moderate non-sterile compounding
    - Making a preparation that requires special calculations or procedures to determine quantities of components per preparation or per individualized dosage units; or making a preparation for which stability data for that specific formulation are not available (USP <795>)
    - Examples of moderate non-sterile compounding include
      - Mixing two or more commercially manufactured creams, ointments, or liquids when the stability of mixture is unknown (IE: Magic or Miracle Mouthwash)
      - Topical preparations intended for local effects
      - Omeprazole suspension when mixed from capsules or active pharmaceutical ingredients (API) since a pH meter is required
      - Preparations requiring special calculations (e.g. salt conversions like valproic acid to sodium valproate)

- Complex non-sterile compounding
  - Compounding of drug preparations which require special training, a special environment or special facilities or equipment or the use of compounding techniques and procedures that may present an elevated risk to the compounder or the patient
  - Examples of complex non-sterile compounding include:
    - NIOSH drug containing preparations or other hazardous agents
    - Radiopharmaceutical preparations
    - Transdermal dosage forms
    - Capsules
    - Suppositories
    - Troches
    - Lollipops
    - Sublingual dosage forms
    - Tablets
    - Tablet triturates
    - Modified-release preparations
    - Other dosage forms intended to deliver systemic effects (inserts, nasal sprays, nasal irrigations, certain gels, etc.)

17 MASSACHUSETTS LAW – COLLABORATIVE PRACTICE

- Collaborative Practice Agreements[33]
  - Pharmacist must:
    - Register with the Department of Public Health and get a controlled substance registration to write prescriptions
    - Maintain $1,000,000 liability insurance
    - Have completed at least 5 years of experience as a pharmacist or residency that the board determines equivalent
    - Participate or apply to participate in MassHealth
  - Collaborative drug therapy management includes the initiating, monitoring, modifying and discontinuing of a patient's drug therapy by a pharmacist in accordance with a collaborative practice agreement
    - Collecting and reviewing patient histories
    - Obtaining and checking vital signs, including pulse, temperature, blood pressure and respiration
    - Under the supervision of, or in direct consultation with, a physician, ordering and evaluating the results of laboratory tests directly related to drug therapy when performed in accordance with approved protocols applicable to the practice setting and when the evaluation shall not include a diagnostic component
    - The pharmacist may order from a drug wholesaler, manufacturer, laboratory or distributor, for purposes of dispensing for immediate treatment, those controlled substances in Schedule VI which the pharmacist is authorized

- Patient must be referred to pharmacist and patient must consent
  - Agreements must include:
    - ✓ Specific disease states being co-managed
    - ✓ Detailed protocols
    - ✓ Detailed procedures for sharing information between provider and pharmacist
  - Must review and renew agreement biennially
  - Pharmacist must keep copy of the agreement, referral, and patient consent readily retrievable in their primary practice setting
    - ✓ The supervising physician must maintain the originals
- Settings in which you can have agreement include:
  - Hospital, long-term care facility, hospice, ambulatory care clinics with on-site supervision by the attending physician
    - ✓ Pharmacist can prescribe using a medication order entered into a patient's medical record
  - Retail pharmacy
    - ✓ Patient must be 18 years of age or older
    - ✓ May administer vaccines
    - ✓ May prescribe an extension by 30 days of current drug therapy prescribed by the supervising physician for not more than two 30-day periods unless otherwise specified
    - ✓ Modification, initiation or discontinuation of medications for:
      - Asthma
      - Chronic obstructive pulmonary disease
      - Diabetes
      - Hypertension
      - Hyperlipidemia
      - Congestive heart failure
      - HIV or AIDS
      - Osteoporosis
    - ✓ No collaborative practice agreement in the retail drug business setting may permit the prescribing of schedule II through V controlled substances
    - ✓ The collaborative practice agreement shall specifically reference each disease state being co-managed
      - May only manage up to 5 different disease states initially
      - The pharmacist must provide a copy of an initial prescription or a modification or discontinuation of a prescription to the supervising physician within 24

hours of its issuance, unless more urgent notification is required under the circumstances
- A community pharmacy cannot hire a physician for the purpose of entering into a collaborative practice agreement but a physician or physician group can hire a pharmacist for collaborative practice
- Each year the pharmacist must complete 5 additional contact hours of Board-approved continuing education (CE) that address the area of practice
  - Keep records of CEs for at least two years after the date of the current collaborative practice agreement

- Expedited Partner Therapy[24]
  - EPT is the practice of treating the sex partners of people diagnosed with Chlamydia infection without examining or testing the partner
  - Healthcare providers may prescribe EPT in two ways:
    - The prescriber provides a prescription for named sex partner(s) of the infected patient; or
    - The prescriber provides a written prescription using "Expedited Partner Therapy," "E.P.T." or "EPT" in place of the patient's name and address
  - The physician, physician assistant, certified nurse practitioner, or nurse midwife counsels the patient about EPT and whenever possible provides the patient with an information sheet provided by the Department, or comparable to that provided by the Department, for the sex partner

18 MASSACHUSETTS LAW – CONTROLLED SUBSTANCES SCHEDULES II TO V

- Controlled Substance Inventories[35]
    - A pharmacist shall keep a perpetual inventory of each CII controlled substance which have been received, dispensed, or disposed of and this inventory must be reconciled every 10 days
    - Must inventory all CII-V on the day you first engage in business
    - Biennially thereafter must inventory all CII-V substances
        - On the same date as the last inventory or within 6 months
    - Inventory newly controlled substances on the day they become scheduled
    - Need records of any CII-V received, distributed, administered, and dispensed
        - The name of the substance and the form of the substance
        - The size of each finished form in metric weight or volume
        - The number of units or volume of each finished form received from other persons; the date received; and the name, address, and Drug Enforcement Administration registration number of the person from whom the substance was received
        - The name, dosage and strength per dosage unit of each controlled substance administered or dispensed; the name and address of the person for whom the controlled substance was administered or dispensed and whether administered or dispensed by delivery or dispensed by prescription; the date of the administration or dispensing, and the written or typewritten name or initials of the person who administered or dispensed the substance

- ➤ The number of units or volume of such finished forms disposed of in any other way by the registrant, including the date and manner of disposal
- Filing
  - Every pharmacy located in a health facility registered with the Commissioner shall file prescriptions for controlled substances as follows:
    - ➤ Prescriptions for controlled substances listed in Schedules I and II shall be filed separately from all other prescriptions of the pharmacy in a file identified for controlled substances listed in Schedules I and II only
    - ➤ Prescriptions for controlled substances listed in Schedules III, IV, and V shall be filed separately from all other prescriptions of the pharmacy in a file identified for controlled substances listed in Schedule III, IV and V only
    - ➤ Prescriptions for controlled substances listed in Schedule VI and prescriptions for non-controlled substances shall be filed separately from all other prescriptions of the pharmacy in a file identified for controlled substances listed in Schedule VI and non-controlled substances

- Massachusetts Prescription Awareness Tool (MassPAT)[36]
  - Prescription Monitoring Program (PMP)
  - Each pharmacy that delivers a schedule II to V controlled substance or a substance classified as an additional drug by the department to the ultimate user shall submit to the department, by electronic means, information regarding each prescription dispensed for a drug including a requirement that each pharmacy collects and reports, for each prescription dispensed a customer identification number and other information associated with the customer identification number
  - Each pharmacy shall submit the information in accordance with transmission methods and frequency requirements promulgated by the department; provided, however, that the information shall be submitted within 24 hours or the next business day. The department may issue a waiver to a pharmacy that is unable to submit prescription information by electronic means
    - ➤ If no controls are filled in that time frame, must submit a "zero report" showing that nothing was dispensed
  - A pharmacy that dispenses a controlled substance must require that a customer identifier is presented whenever a controlled substance in Schedules II through V, or an additional drug (IE: gabapentin) is dispensed

- ▲ Must check that the ID is valid and not out of date
- ▲ A customer identifier is defined as the identification number on a valid government-issued ID, including state-issued ID, military ID cards, permanent resident cards, passports, driver's licenses, Massachusetts Commission for the Blind ID cards, or other ID as specified by the Massachusetts Department of Public Health
- ▲ The pharmacy may dispense medication to the patient or the patient's representative. For example, a parent may pick up a prescription for a child or a relative may pick up a prescription for a housebound family member. The pharmacy must check the ID of the person picking up the prescription
- ▫ The pharmacy may dispense a controlled substance in Schedules II through V or an additional drug without reviewing the customer identifier if the pharmacy has reason to believe that the failure to dispense the controlled substance or additional drug would result in a serious hardship for the ultimate user or agent of the ultimate user, and documents the reason; and the ultimate user or agent of the ultimate user prints his or her name and address on the reverse side of the prescription and signs his or her name thereto, or in the case of an electronic prescription, provides an electronic signature; and the pharmacy provides to the Department those informational fields required by the Department
  - ▲ The pharmacist enters "cust signed rx" in the PMP customer ID field (AIR05) rather than leaving the field blank
- ▫ When a pharmacy delivers in person or through a common carrier to a private residence or to a facility where the patient is located, MA PMP does not require the pharmacy to collect and report a customer ID. The pharmacy will use its internal procedures for tracking deliveries. When submitting data utilizing the "deliveries exception," pharmacies should populate the relevant fields as follows:
  - ▲ PAT21 [Patient Location Code] – The pharmacist should use his/her professional judgment to determine which of the available location codes applies. Be as accurate as possible in selecting the code. Do not leave the field blank
  - ▲ AIR05 [Customer ID] - Enter "delivery"
  - ▲ AIR06 [Relationship of the customer to the patient] – Enter '99'
- ▫ Every registered practitioner except veterinarians who has a MCSR will automatically be granted authority to utilize the prescription monitoring program

- Practitioner must check:
  - Each time prescribing any narcotic drug in Schedule II or III or a benzodiazepine
  - Prior to prescribing a Schedule IV or V controlled substance "as designated in guidance to be issued by the Department" to a patient for the first time
- Exceptions:
  - If prescriber has been granted a waiver
    - ✓ For hardship, technology issues
  - If treating a hospice patient
  - If treating patient in Emergency Department and
    - ✓ Prescriber doesn't anticipate prescribing CII-V or
    - ✓ Does not prescribe more than a 5-day supply of a CII-V
  - Emergency care where it could result in patient harm by delaying care
  - If treating a hospital inpatient
  - Single dose or small quantity medications for immediate treatment dispensed by the provider
  - When system is down or it is not possible to use it due to temporary technological failure
  - Patients younger than 8 years old
- Primary account holder can give delegate an account under them as long as the delegate is not eligible for their own account
  - The primary account holder is responsible for all delegate use
- Department can suspend an account holder's use of the program for improper use

19 MASSACHUSETTS LAW – MISCELLANEOUS

- Automated Pharmacy System[37]
  - Prior to using an automated pharmacy system, a pharmacy is required to:
    - Notify the Board and the Department in writing of the intent to use an automated pharmacy system, including the name and address of the pharmacy location, the hours of operation of the system, the type or name of the system, and a description of how the system is used by pharmacy
    - Develop and maintain on-site a policy and procedure manual
      - Name and address of the pharmacy where the automated pharmacy system is being used
      - Manufacturer's name, model, and serial number or other identifying nomenclature of the system
      - Description of how the system is used by the pharmacy
      - Quality assurance procedures to determine continued appropriate use of the system
      - Policies and procedures for system operation, safety, security, accountability, accuracy, patient confidentiality, access (multilingual capabilities recommended) and malfunction, with requirement that any malfunction of the system shall be reported immediately to the Pharmacist-in-Charge for corrective action
      - Procedures related to identification and analysis of any system dispensing error

- Patient Consultation and Patient Choice
  - A pharmacy or Pharmacist-in-Charge shall establish policies and procedures that ensure that the automated pharmacy system used by the pharmacy:
    - Only contains Schedule VI controlled substance medication for REFILL prescriptions that:
      - Do not require oral consultation by law
      - Are properly labeled and verified by a pharmacist before placement into the automated pharmacy system and subsequent release to pharmacy customers
      - Allows a patient to choose whether or not to use the system
      - Provides opportunity for a patient to consult with a pharmacist during any hours that prescriptions are available for pickup from the automated dispensing system
- Security
  - An automated pharmacy system must be secured against or within the wall or floor in a manner that prevents unauthorized removal of the system. A pharmacy must have written policies and procedures that provide for adequate security systems and procedures that:
    - Provide a method to identify the patient and only release that patient's prescription
    - Ensure system methods to prevent unauthorized access
- Records
  - An automated pharmacy system must maintain records and electronic data that include the following information:
    - Name of providing pharmacy
    - Prescription number
    - Name, strength, dosage form, and quantity of the drug accessed
    - Name of the patient for whom the drug was ordered
    - Date and time of dispensing
    - Name of prescribing practitioner
    - Identity of the pharmacist who approved the prescription order
    - Identity of the person to whom the drug was released

- Access
  - Access to and limits on access (e.g., security levels) to the automated pharmacy system must be established by policy and procedures that comply with state and federal regulations and provide adequate security to prevent unauthorized individuals from accessing or obtaining drugs or devices
    - The Pharmacist-in-Charge shall have sole responsibility to:
      - Assign, discontinue, or change access to the system
      - Ensure that access to system drugs or devices is restricted to authorized licensed personnel for the purposes of administration based on a valid prescription order
      - Ensure that the automated pharmacy system is stocked accurately and in accordance with written policies and procedures
- Stocking and Returning Medication
  - The stocking and return of all prescription medications in the automated pharmacy system shall:
    - Only be completed by a pharmacist, intern, or certified pharmacy technician
    - Be recorded and maintained in the system and include identification of the person(s) authorized to stock medication and perform accuracy checks of the system stock
    - Be limited to medications not requiring refrigeration or reconstitution, which are packaged and labeled in accordance with federal and state laws and regulations
    - Include procedures for securing and accounting for prescription medications removed from and subsequently returned to pharmacy stock
    - Include procedures for securing and accounting for wasted prescription medications or discarded medications and well as product recalls generated by manufacturer, distributor, or pharmacy, in accordance with existing regulations
    - Utilize two separate verifications, such as bar code verification, electronic verification, weight verification, radio frequency identification (RFID) or similar process, to ensure that the proper medication is dispensed from the system

- Shared Pharmacy Service Models Including Central Fill, Central and Remote Processing, and Telepharmacy
    - Shared Pharmacy Services are defined by the NABP as a system that allows a participating pharmacist or pharmacy, pursuant to a request from another participating pharmacist or pharmacy, to process or fill a prescription drug order, which may include preparing, packaging, labeling, compounding for specific patients, dispensing, performing Drug Utilization Reviews, conducting claims adjudication, obtaining refill authorizations, reviewing therapeutic interventions, and/or reviewing institutional facility orders
    - Shared Pharmacy Service
        - All licensees must maintain full compliance with all federal and state laws and regulations while implementing and utilizing Shared Pharmacy Service models
        - Pharmacies dispensing medication into or from Massachusetts must possess a license issued by the Board
        - Pharmacies engaged in Shared Service models must:
            - ✓ Have the same owner; or
            - ✓ Have a written contract or agreement that outlines the services provided and the shared responsibilities of each party
        - Pharmacy systems must have the ability to track and produce an audit trail of the prescription during each step in the pharmacy process to include at a minimum: date/time and individuals involved
        - Each Board licensee engaging in Shared Pharmacy Services is jointly responsible for properly processed and filled prescriptions
        - Shared Pharmacy Service models must not compromise initiation or continuation of patient therapy, quality, or safety
        - Retail pharmacies must notify patients that their prescription drug orders may be processed or filled by another pharmacy
        - All personnel engaged in Shared Pharmacy Services must have documented training
        - Patient must be allowed to opt out
        - Review policies annually and document review
        - Pharmacies must establish and maintain a continuity of care plan outlining how patients' prescription needs will be met in the event that any Shared Pharmacy Services participant is unable to process or fill patient prescriptions

- Central fill
  - A pharmacy licensed by the Board planning to serve as a central fill pharmacy for other pharmacies must file a petition to the Board and receive the Board's approval prior to engaging in any central filling activities
  - Any central fill pharmacy dispensing medications into or from Massachusetts to participating pharmacies must be licensed in Massachusetts
  - CII-V must go back to originating pharmacy to dispense to patient
  - CVI, with the exception of drugs requiring reporting to MassPAT (PMP), may be delivered or shipped directly to the patient from the central fill pharmacy
  - Unless otherwise approved by the Board, the central filling of compounded sterile preparations or complex non-sterile preparations to be dispensed into or from Massachusetts is not permitted
- Central and remote processing
  - A system that allows the processing of patient-specific prescriptions for a Massachusetts licensed pharmacy without final product verification or dispensing responsibilities
  - Prescriptions may be processed outside the premises of a licensed Massachusetts pharmacy provided that the processes are verified by a Massachusetts licensed pharmacist or performed in a pharmacy licensed by the Board
    - ✓ Pharmacy technicians may perform remote processing of prescriptions on behalf of a retail or institutional pharmacy that is located in Massachusetts without the on-site supervision by a Board-licensed pharmacist provided they hold a Massachusetts pharmacy technician license
- Telepharmacy
  - The scope of telepharmacy allowed by this policy is limited to:
    - ✓ Remote pharmacist verification of the final patient-specific product utilizing telepharmacy technologies
    - ✓ Clinical activities conducted by a pharmacist such as patient counseling, drug utilization review, and drug therapy monitoring utilizing telepharmacy technologies
  - Remote verification is ok but you need at least one pharmacist on the premise where dispensing
  - Telepharmacy activities allowed by this policy must be conducted by a Massachusetts licensed pharmacist or performed in a pharmacy licensed by the Board

20 REFERENCE CHARTS

Records Reference Chart

Name of Record	How Long to Keep	Reference
Controlled substance reports, inventories, records	2 years	105 CMR 700.006
Controlled substance prescriptions	2 years	M.G.L. c. 94C section 23
Transfer of controlled substances	2 years	247 CMR 6.10
Quality Related Events report	2 years	247 CMR 15.00
Improper dispensing leading to death/serious injury	2 years from date report is filed with the board	247 CMR 6.14
Automated Dispensing Device (ADD) records	2 years	Joint Policy 2019-02: Automated Dispensing Device Use
Documentation of CEs	2 years from date of completion	247 CMR 4.06
Transferred prescriptions	2 years from the date of last refill	247 CMR 9.02
Radiopharmaceutical records	3 years	247 CMR 13.00
Defective drug preparation log	10 years	M.G.L. c. 112 sections 39D

Report Reference Chart

Name of Report	How Long You Have to Submit	Reference
Change in pharmacy corporate structure of owners	10 working days	247 CMR 6.03
Registered pharmacist starting or terminating employment	10 working days	247 CMR 6.03
Change in pharmacist mailing address	10 working days	247 CMR 6.05
Change in pharmacist name	10 working days	247 CMR 6.05
Termination as pharmacy MOR	10 working days	247 CMR 6.07
Closing of pharmacy	14 days prior by certified mail	247 CMR 6.09
Copy of transfer inventory from closing pharmacy	10 days	247 CMR 6.10
After closing a pharmacy: return permit, CSR, certificate of fitness and dispose of controlled substances	10 days	247 CMR 6.09
Death/serious injury from improper dispensing	15 business days	247 CMR 6.14
Deficiency during inspection by BOP	15 business days to submit written plan of correction	247 CMR 6.13
All non-routine notices, correspondence, disciplinary actions, adverse changes in accreditation from other entities	7 business days	247 CMR 6.15

Name of Report	How Long You Have to Submit	Reference
Errors relating to USP 797 (sterility/USP issues, environmental problems, failure of environmental certifications)	7 business days	247 CMR 6.15
Retail and Institutional Sterile Pharmacy – total number and type of prescriptions dispensed, states dispensed to, non-resident license statuses, hood certifications, ISO certifications	Every 6 months	247 CMR 6.15(5)
Retail and Institutional Sterile Pharmacy – list of scripts dispensed, volume, names of states shipped to if applicable	Annually	M.G.L. c. 112 section 39G and I
Retail Complex Non-Sterile Pharmacy – list of scripts dispensed, volume, names of states shipped to if applicable	Annually	M.G.L. c. 112 sections 39H
Total number of Emergency Contraceptives dispensed pursuant to standing order	Annually by August 1 for time frame July 1 to June 30	MGL c. 94C, 19A
Total number of Naloxone doses dispensed and how many were paid for by insurance	Annually, by January 15th	2018-04: Naloxone Dispensing via Standing Order
Possible loss of a controlled substance (to the DEA)	1 business day	DEA Pharmacist's Manual
Loss of a controlled substance DEA Form 106 (to the DEA)	No set time frame but as soon as possible – should provide DEA with updates when possible	DEA Pharmacist's Manual
Possible loss of controlled substance (to BOP)	7 business days	Policy 2018-05 247 CMR 6.02(10)
Outcome of investigation of loss or theft (to BOP)	Within 21 days of initial notification	Policy 2018-05 247 CMR 6.02(10)

Name of Report	How Long You Have to Submit	Reference
Confirmed theft or loss (to BOP using DEA form 106)	Within 7 business days of confirmed loss	Policy 2018-05 247 CMR 6.02(10)
Insignificant loss	Does not need to be reported but must be documented onsite	Policy 2018-05 247 CMR 6.02(10)
Losses resulting from confirmed dispensing error	Does not need to be reported	Policy 2018-05 247 CMR 6.02(10)
Loss of a controlled substance (DEA form 106) (to the state police for a distributer or to the town <u>and</u> state police for a dispenser)	Simultaneously when you send report to DEA	M.G.L. c. 94C section 15
Change in name or address for Controlled Substance Registration	Apply for new registration up to 90 days in advance of change	105 CMR 700.004 (J1)
Termination of registration for Controlled Substance Registration	Notify 30 days in advance – surrender by mailing to Commissioner	105 CMR 700.004 (J2)
Disclosure of Above Action Level Environmental Monitoring (EM) Results Form 1: Initial Reporting Form	Within 7 days of notification of result	Policy 2019-08: Sterile Compounding Pharmacy Response to Above Action Level Environmental Monitoring Results
Disclosure of Above Action Level Environmental Monitoring (EM) Results Form 2: Final Reporting Form	Within 21 days of initial reporting	Policy 2019-08: Sterile Compounding Pharmacy

Misc. Time Frame Reference Chart

Name	Time Frame	Reference
Length of time you must maintain a patient's medication record for from the date of last entry	12 months (except as otherwise required federal law)	247 CMR 9.07
Supply of medication allowed to be dispensed from veterinarian emergency kit	120-hour supply	Joint Policy 2019-06: Compounded Emergency Medications for Veterinarian Use
Inspect, reconcile, restock veterinarian emergency kit	At least every 10 days	Joint Policy 2019-06: Compounded Emergency Medications for Veterinarian Use
Absence time frame to appoint an interim manager	>30 days absence <100 days absence	98-010: Policy on Extended Leave
Absence time frame to submit a new application for a change in Manager-of-Record	≥100 day absence	98-010: Policy on Extended Leave

Name	Time Frame	Reference
Reconciliation of perpetual CII inventory	Every 10 days	Policy 2018-05 Appendix I 247 CMR 6.02(10)
Maximum day supply a hospital pharmacy can fill for an emergency room or discharge patient	14 days (unless manufacturer only supplies in larger quantity then can fill for minimum quantity supplied)	105 CMR 722.090
Maximum day supply of script that can be filled after discontinuance of provider's practice	30-day supply at a time up to a maximum of one 90-day supply total (can fill one 90-day supply only if insurance requires)	2005-01: Continuation of drug therapy upon discontinuance of a practitioner's practice
How often you must review and renew collaborative practice agreement	Biennially	M.G.L. c. 112 section 24B

SELECT REFERENCES:

1. e-CFR Title 21, Chapter I, Subchapter C, Part 201
2. Title 16, Volume II, Subchapter E, Part 1700
3. DEA Pharmacist's Manual
4. 105 CMR 700, M.G.L. c. 94C section 31
5. Circular Letter: DCP 19-12-108, 105 CMR 721.020, 247 CMR 5.00, M.G.L. c. 94C section 20/23
6. M.G.L. c. 94C section 22, 105 CMR 721.020
7. M.G.L. c. 94C Section 27
8. M.G.L. c. 94C section 31
9. M.G.L. c. 94C Section 18
10. 247 CMR 9.02, Policy 2019-04: Transfer of Unfilled Prescriptions
11. M.G.L. c. 94C section 21
12. M.G.L. c. 94C section 21A, 247 CMR 9.07(3)
13. M.G.L. c. 94C section 7, 105 CMR 700.004
14. 2011-02: License Reinstatement Following Surrender, Suspension, or Revocation, 247 CMR 4.02
15. Policy 2018-03, 247 CMR 4.03
16. 247 CMR 2.00, Reference: M.G.L. c. 112 section 24G, 2021-01: Pharmacy Intern Supervision and Dedicated Training Personnel
17. Policy 2000-03
18. 247 CMR 6.00
19. M.G.L. c. 94C section 21B
20. 247 CMR 6.09
21. 105 CMR 722.090
22. Circular Letter: DHCQ 18-6-679
23. Circular Letter: DHCQ 20-3-700
24. 247 CMR 13.00
25. 247 CMR 21.00
26. Board Policy No. 2006-1 Joint guidelines regarding pharmacist dispensing of Emergency Contraception, M.G.L. c. 94C section 19ABC, 2018-04: Naloxone Dispensing via Standing Order, Circular: DCP 19-6-107, 105 CMR 700.004
27. M.G.L. c. 94C section 34A
28. Policy 2018-05, DEA Pharmacist's manual
29. 247 CMR 15.00
30. Policy 2020-02: Compounding of Commercially Available Drugs
31. Policy 2019-08
32. 247 CMR 18.00
33. M.G.L. c. 112 section 24B, 105 CMR 700.003 I, 246 CMR 16.00
34. Policy 2015-03, 105 CMR 700.003J
35. 105 CMR 700.006, 247 CMR 9.01(14)
36. 247 CMR 700.012 (3), MGL c. 94C section 24a, 105 CMR 700.012G
37. 2010-02 Joint Guidelines for the Use of Automated Pharmacy Systems for the Storage and Dispensing of Schedule VI Controlled Substance Prescriptions in Pharmacies, 2021-02: Shared Pharmacy Service Models Including Central Fill, Central and Remote Processing, and Telepharmacy

Made in United States
North Haven, CT
13 October 2021